SINGER

SEWING REFERENCE LIBRARY®

Sewing
for Children

CREATIVE
PUBLISHING
international

MINNETONKA, MINNESOTA

SINGER

SEWING REFERENCE LIBRARY®

Sewing
for Children

Contents

How to Use This Book 7

CREATIVE
PUBLISHING
international

President/CEO: David D. Murphy
Vice President/Editorial: Patricia K. Jacobsen
Vice President/Retail Sales & Marketing:
  Richard M. Miller

Library of Congress Cataloging-in-Publication Data
Sewing for children.
     p. cm. -- (Singer sewing reference library)
   Includes index.
   ISBN 0-86573-174-8 (softcover)
  1. Children's clothing. 2. Children's paraphernalia. 3. Machine
sewing. I. Creative Publishing international. II. Series.

TT635.S475 1999
646.4'06--dc21   99-34194

Copyright © 1999
Creative Publishing international, Inc.
5900 Green Oak Drive
Minnetonka, Minnesota 55343
1-800-328-3895
All rights reserved
Printed in U.S.A.

Books available in this series:
Sewing Essentials, Sewing for the Home, Clothing Care & Repair, Sewing for Style, Sewing Specialty Fabrics, Sewing Activewear, The Perfect Fit, Timesaving Sewing, More Sewing for the Home, Tailoring, 101 Sewing Secrets, Sewing Pants That Fit, Decorative Machine Stitching, Creative Sewing Ideas, Sewing Lingerie, Sewing Projects for the Home, Sewing with Knits, More Creative Sewing Ideas, Quilt Projects by Machine, Creating Fashion Accessories, Quick & Easy Sewing Projects, Sewing for Special Occasions, Sewing for the Holidays, Quick & Easy Decorating Projects, Quilted Projects & Garments, Embellished Quilted Projects, Window Treatments, Holiday Projects, Halloween Costumes, Upholstery Basics, Fabric Artistry, The New Sewing with a Serger, The New Quilting by Machine

SEWING FOR CHILDREN

Created by: The Editors of Creative
Publishing international, Inc. in
cooperation with the Sewing Education
Department, Singer Sewing Company.
Singer is a trademark of The Singer
Company Limited and is used under
license.

Executive Editor: Elaine Perry
Project Managers: Linnéa Christensen,
  Amy Friebe
Senior Editor: Linda Neubauer
Art Directors: Stephanie Michaud,
  Delores Swanson
Project & Prop Stylist: Joanne Wawra
Lead Samplemaker: Phyllis Galbraith

Sewing Staff: Arlene Dohrman, Sharon
  Ecklund, Bridget Haugh, Teresa Henn
Studio Services Manager: Marcia Chambers
Photo Services Coordinator: Carol Osterhus
Senior Lead Photographer: Chuck Nields
Photographer: Andrea Rugg
Desktop Publishing Specialist:
  Laurie Kristensen
Publishing Production Manager: Kim Gerber
Production Staff: Patrick Gibson,
  Laura Hokkanen, Helga Thielen
Consultants: Kitty Benton, Virginia Carney,
  Jana Davis, Zoe Graul, Vicki Hastings,
  Carol Jones, Jackie Kanthak, JoAnn Krause,
  Christine Nelson, Melanie Nelson-Smith,
  Barbara Palmer, Kathy Sandmann,
  Mary Pat Sweetman
Contributing Manufacturers: B. Blumenthal &
  Co., Inc.; Butterick Company, Inc.; Clotilde;

Coats & Clark; Daisy Kingdom, Inc.;
Dritz Corporation; Dyno Merchandise
Corporation; EZ International;
Freudenberg, Pellon Division; June Tailor,
Inc.; Kwik Sew Pattern Company; The
McCall Pattern Company; Minnetonka
Mills, Inc.; Olfa Productions Corporation;
Rowenta, Inc.; Sew Easy Textiles, Inc.;
Simplicity Pattern Company, Inc.; The
Singer Company; Speed Stitch, Inc.; Stacy
Industries, Inc.; Stretch & Sew, Inc.;
Sunrise Industries, Inc.; Swiss-Metrosene,
Inc.; Vin Max, Inc.; YKK Home Sewing
Division

Printed on American paper by:
R. R. Donnelley & Sons Co.
10 9 8 7 6 5 4 3 2

How to Use This Book

Sewing for Children will help you sew customized, professional-quality children's garments and room decor easily and quickly. Use this book to plan and sew attractive clothing and accessories for infants, toddlers, and school-age children. Garments should be comfortable, durable, and becoming to the child.

Sewing for Children contains complete and detailed instructions for some projects; for others, it gives helpful hints and creative ideas.

Most children's clothing has less detail than adult clothing and can be sewn in a shorter period of time. Many of the projects in this book are excellent starting points for the novice sewer or for someone who has not sewn for a number of years. Experienced sewers will find helpful shortcuts and suggestions for pattern variations or adaptations.

To make the most efficient use of your time, become familiar with information in the Getting Started section of the book before you select a project. Learn about up-to-date equipment, notions, fabrics, patterns, and styles. Sewing techniques for the serger, or overlock machine, are included where appropriate. When a serging method is shown, a conventional sewing machine method is also suggested.

Directions for specific methods are given step-by-step, with close-up photographs for explicit detail. In some photographs, contrasting thread is used to highlight the sewing technique, but you will want to use matching thread for your own projects, unless contrasting thread is desired for a decorative effect.

Sewing for Children's Changing Needs

Making clothing for children is different from sewing for adults. Although children's clothing requires less fitting, children grow quickly and have different clothing needs at different ages. Use the Infants section

for planning and sewing a layette. You may also want to choose specific projects, ranging from receiving blankets and bibs to kimonos and buntings.

The Growing Up section of the book covers activewear for toddlers and children. Included are tips for adding durability and room for growth to garments you sew. You will also find many creative ideas for making a garment special. To get the most versatility and use from garments you sew for a child, follow the wardrobe planning tips to coordinate garments. As children begin dressing themselves and selecting their own clothes, they often express strong preferences; you may want to involve the child in the planning when choosing colors, styles, and fabrics.

Using Your Creativity

Some of the ideas in this book are as simple as using a unique notion or closure. In the Personalizing section, we have included several techniques for adding a personal touch to a garment by sewing a patchwork border, mixing fabrics creatively, or using the artistic ideas of the child who will wear the garment. Many of these personalizing techniques are not limited to the garments that you sew, but can also be used to customize T-shirts and other purchased clothing. With the help of *Sewing for Children*, you can sew more creatively by customizing children's clothing.

The Bedroom Decorating section of the book includes creative projects and ideas for sewing an entire crib ensemble, padded wall sculptures, and easy unique window toppers. Choose fabrics in colors and patterns that fill your child's bedroom with personality and cheerfulness. With your sewing machine and a little ingenuity, you can create designer bedroom decor at a bargain price.

Getting Started

Choosing Children's Clothing

Sewing children's clothes can be quite economical and need not be time-consuming. Because children's garments require less fabric than garments for adults, the fabric cost is usually minimal. You may be able to use fabric from other sewing projects to construct a garment, or part of a garment, for a young child.

Most children's clothing designs follow simple lines, have few pieces, and are easy to sew. They are a good starting point for a beginning sewer or for a sewer whose skills need updating.

Planning for Safety

Build safety into children's garments. Avoid loose strings or excess fabric that may get tangled, especially for infants. Beware of long skirts or gowns that may cause a child to trip, or very full sleeves that may catch on objects. Limit tie belts and drawstrings to short lengths, and securely fasten buttons and trims. Use fire-retardant fabrics for sleepwear.

Customizing Clothes for Children

Creative touches can make a garment special to a child. Use a child's crayon drawing as a guide to colors and shapes for a machine-embroidered design. Or let children color or paint fabric before you cut out the pattern. Some children may enjoy designing their clothes by drawing the garment they would like and then having you match the color and general style. Simple, original appliqués can reflect a favorite hobby or special toy.

Involve the child in selecting patterns, fabrics, and notions. For young children learning to identify colors, primary colors of red, yellow, and blue are popular. Look at colors of a favorite toy and the colors a child often chooses for painting or drawing. Consider the coloring of the child's hair, eyes, and skin; select colors that compliment them.

Features for Self-dressing

To encourage self-dressing, choose garments with loose-fitting necklines and waistlines and with manageable fasteners. Make closures easy to see and reach on the front or side of a garment. Hook and loop tape can be used for closures on most types of garments. Young children can easily unfasten simple, large, round buttons and snaps, but may have difficulty closing them with small hands. They also enjoy smooth-running zippers with large teeth and zipper pulls. Pull-on pants that have elastic waists are easier for young children to pull on and off. Children can be frustrated by trying to fasten hooks and eyes, tiny buttons, and ties.

Tips for Planning Garments for Growth and Comfort

Add ribbing cuffs to lower edges of sleeves or pants legs so you can turn up built-in room for growth.

Choose pants patterns in a style that can be cut off for shorts when outgrown in length.

Use elastic waists on generously sized pants or skirts for comfort during growth spurts.

Allow extra crotch and body length in one-piece garments to prevent them from becoming uncomfortable as the child grows.

Add elastic suspenders with adjustable closures.

Choose dress and jumper patterns with dropped waist or no waist for comfort and maximum length of wear.

Use knit fabrics for easier sewing and maximum stretch for growth and comfort.

Consider patterns with pleats, gathers, and wide shapes that allow for growth without riding up.

Select patterns with raglan, dolman, and dropped sleeves to offer room for growth and less restriction of movement.

Select oversized styles for comfort.

Selecting Patterns

All children are comfortable in loose-fitting garments, but their clothing requirements change as they grow. For infants, select one-piece garments, such as kimonos, that make it easy to dress the baby and change the diapers. Toddlers are also comfortable in one-piece garments, such as overalls, with a crotch opening. Two-piece styles with elastic waistbands are easy to get on and off and are practical for children who are being toilet-trained. Adjustable shoulder straps and straps that crisscross at the back, as well as elastic waistbands, help keep pants and skirts in place.

Look for basic, versatile styles. Coordinated pants, shirts, skirts, jackets, overalls, and sweatsuits can be worn year-round. Except for skirts, these garments can be worn by both boys and girls. Use a basic pattern to plan a mix-and-match wardrobe. Coordinate fabrics and notions, and save time by sewing several garments, using the same pattern.

Selecting a Pattern Size

Buy patterns according to the child's measurements, not the child's age or ready-to-wear size. Compare the child's measurements with the chart on the pattern or in a pattern catalog. Most pattern measurement charts are standardized; however, the fit of similar garments may vary, even though the same size pattern is used. The style of the garment, whether it is loose-fitting or close-fitting, and the amount of ease added for movement and comfort affect the fit.

You may want to compare the pattern with a well-fitting garment to check the fit of the garment you intend to make. If the child is between two sizes, buy the larger size pattern. Multi-sized patterns can be used for several sizes. To preserve the original pattern, trace each size as it is used.

To reflect the changing shape of growing bodies, pattern sizes for different ages use different body measurements. Infants' patterns give the baby's length and weight. Toddlers' patterns give chest, waist, and approximate height measurements. The Toddlers' sizes are shorter in length than Children's sizes and have extra room for diapers. Children's sizes give measurements for chest, waist, hip, and approximate height. Up to a size 6, Children's patterns generally increase one size for each additional inch (2.5 cm) around the body.

Fitting

Most children's garments require minimal fitting. Even if some of the child's measurements differ slightly from those on the pattern, you may not need to make adjustments. For example, a garment with elastic at the waist may not need a waistline adjustment. Determine adjustments before cutting the fabric. Make the same amount of adjustment to adjoining pattern pieces, and preserve the grainline on the adjusted pattern. You can make some adjustments as you sew by using wider or narrower seam allowances.

Adjusting Pattern Length and Width

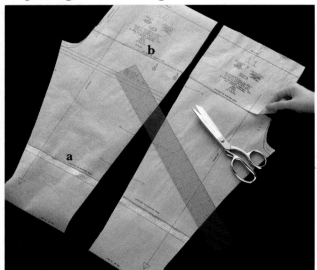

Lengthen (a) or shorten (b) pattern at adjustment lines. Spread or lap pattern pieces to desired adjustment; tape, preserving grainline. Blend the cutting and stitching lines.

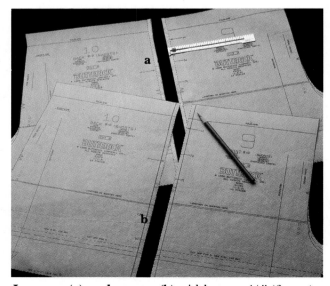

Increase (a) or decrease (b) width up to ¼" (6 mm) on each side seam allowance for total adjustment up to 1" (2.5 cm). To increase or decrease width more than 1" (2.5 cm), use different pattern size. On bodices, you will need to adjust ease in sleeve to fit new armhole size.

Taking Measurements

To take a child's measurements, use a tape measure or brightly colored nonstretch ribbon held snugly, but not tightly. The child should wear underwear or diapers and stand in a natural position. For a very young or active child, you can measure a garment that fits well and compare it with the garment size on the pattern envelope. You will not need all measurements every time you sew.

Head. Measure around the fullest part of the head. This measurement is important for garments without neckline plackets.

Chest. Measure around the fullest part of the chest, just over the shoulder blades.

Waist. Toddlers often do not have a distinct waistline. To determine the natural waistline, tie a string around the midsection; have the child move and bend. The string will fall into place; measure over the string.

Hips. Measure around the fullest part of the hips.

Back waist length. Measure from the prominent bone at the neck to the natural waistline; you can locate the neckbone when the child's head is bent forward.

Arm-across-back length. With the child's arm extended straight out at the side, measure from the wrist across the shoulder to the middle of the neck. Place the sleeve pattern next to the garment back pattern, overlapping seam allowances; measure pattern from wrist to center back. You can now compare the body measurement with the pattern measurement.

Crotch depth. Tie a string around the waist. Have the child sit on a chair; measure at the side from the waist to the seat of the chair.

Finished dress or skirt length. Measure from a string at the waist to the desired hem length.

Finished pants length. Measure from a string at the waist to the anklebone.

Selecting Fabrics

Children's everyday garments need to withstand the wear and tear of active play and numerous launderings. For these clothes, select durable, comfortable, easy-care fabrics. For special-occasion clothing, use washable velveteens and taffetas or fine-wale corduroys.

Natural fibers are soft and non-abrasive. They offer breathability and moisture absorption, qualities lacking in pure synthetics; but natural fibers may require more care. Synthetic fibers, such as acrylic and polyester, are easy-care, but they do not breathe or absorb moisture. They stain easily, and with repeated launderings they eventually pill, yellow, and lose their softness. Blends of natural and synthetic fibers combine the best properties of each to produce soft, absorbent, wrinkle-free fabrics.

Fabric Types

Woven fabrics that are lightweight are suitable for blouses, shirts, dresses, and skirts. Firmly woven fabrics are most durable; choose them for pants, shirts, and jackets. Woven fabrics best suited for sewing children's clothing are batiste, broadcloth, chambray, chino, denim, dotted Swiss, duck, gingham, madras, organdy, polyester taffeta, poplin, sailcloth, seersucker, shirting, twill, and voile.

Knit fabrics are a good choice, because children are active and knits give as the body moves. When selecting knits, check the stretch of the fabric with the gauge on the pattern envelope. Knit fabrics include: cotton spandex, double knit, interlock, jersey, sweatshirt fleece, and thermal knit.

Fabrics with nap have a surface texture that feels soft or brushed, and may be either woven or knit. These fabrics include: brushed denim, corduroy, flannel, French terry, synthetic fleece, piqué, stretch terry, terry cloth, velveteen, and velour.

Fabrics for children's clothing include: broadcloth in solid colors or small prints **(1)**, denim **(2)**, velour **(3)**, corduroy **(4)**, terry cloth **(5)**, interlock **(6)**, jersey **(7)**, dotted Swiss **(8)**, and synthetic fleece **(9)**.

Decorative Trims

Decorative trims for garments and room accessories are available for purchase by the yard (meter) or in prepackaged lengths. Lace and eyelet edgings, featuring one decorative edge, come in flat or pre-gathered styles. Narrow ribbons and braids with designs on the right side are edgestitched to clothing or accessories. Thin piping, in solid colors or stripes, is stitched into garment seams. Thicker fabric-covered cording is used to accent and support seams of room accessories, like bumper pads or pillows. Rick rack, in several sizes and colors, is topstitched down the center or stitched into seams.

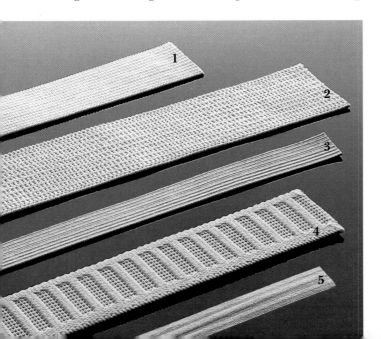

Elastic

Elastics vary in stretch and recovery characteristics. Look for elastics that retain their original width when stretched and that recover to their original length when applied to a garment. Those made from cotton and rubber are the most durable.

Knitted (1) and woven (2) elastics are most appropriate for stitching directly to the garment. Braided (3) and nonroll (4) elastic are suitable for casings. Transparent (5) elastic blends with any fabric color and is comfortable next to the skin.

Ribbing

The stretch and recovery of ribbing varies widely. The stretch is acceptable if a 4" (10 cm) piece stretches fully to about 7" (18 cm).

The finished width of ribbing is in proportion to the garment edge and size. Cut the ribbing twice the finished width plus ½" (1.3 cm) for two ¼" (6 mm) seam allowances. Trim the garment seam allowances to ¼" (6 mm) on edges where ribbing will be applied. Use the method below to cut ribbing to fit the edge of the garment. Or, for a closer fit at wrist, waistline, and pants leg, cut the ribbing to fit the body. It may then be necessary to gather the garment edge to fit the ribbing.

Tubular ribbing is 18" to 22" (46 to 56 cm) wide and is sold by the inch (2.5 cm). It is available in two weights. The lighter weight is suitable for use on T-shirt knits, sweatshirt fleece, velours, and lightweight woven fabrics. The heavier weight is used for outerwear or heavyweight fabrics. Do not preshrink ribbing; this distorts the ribbing and makes accurate layout and cutting difficult.

Guide to Cut Width of Ribbings (includes seam allowances)

Garment Edge	Infants'	Toddlers'	Children's
Short sleeve	2" (5 cm)	2½" (6.5 cm)	2½" (6.5 cm)
Standard crew neck	2½" (6.5 cm)	2½" (6.5 cm)	3" (7.5 cm)
Narrow crew neck	2" (5 cm)	2" (5 cm)	2½" (6.5 cm)
Prefinished collar	2½" (6.5 cm)	2¾" (7 cm)	3" (7.5 cm)
Waistband, wrists, pants legs	4¼" (10.8 cm)	5" (12.5 cm)	6½" (16.3 cm)
Pocket	2" (5 cm)	2" (5 cm)	2½" (6.5 cm)

How to Measure and Cut Ribbing

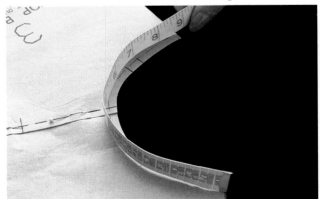

1) Measure pattern edge where ribbing is to be applied, standing tape measure on edge at seamline. For neck and waist edges, double this measurement.

2) Cut ribbing two-thirds the measured length of seamline and twice desired finished width; add ½" (1.3 cm) to length and width for seam allowances.

Equipment & Tools

A conventional sewing machine with basic utility stitches works well for sewing children's clothing, although a machine with embroidery capabilities can be helpful for adding embellishments. For small, hard-to-reach areas, such as knees and elbows, a free-arm sewing machine is useful. A serger does not replace a conventional machine, but it can cut sewing time considerably; it sews a seam at the same time it finishes and trims the edges. Sergers can also be used to stitch hems often used in ready-to-wear clothes.

Ballpoint needles (1) are used for sewing knits. Universal point needles (2) are designed to be used with knits or woven fabrics. Twin needles (3) work well for reinforcement stitches as well as hems. Metalfil® needles (4) are designed for machine embroidery.

A general purpose presser foot (5) is used for most steps of the construction process, including straight stitching and zigzagging. A special-purpose foot (6), or embroidery foot is used for sewing repetitive satin stitch designs. The wide groove on the underside of the foot allows it to ride smoothly over the raised stitches. A zipper foot (7) is necessary for stitching close to the zipper teeth; it is also helpful for sewing seams that are accented with piping or fabric-covered cording.

A bodkin (8) is a long metal or plastic tool that is handy for threading elastic, ribbon, or cord through a casing. A rotary cutter (9) and cutting mat (10) are handy for cutting out garments. The cutter is available in two sizes and comes with a retractable blade for safety. There is also a rotary cutter with a wave blade (11), for cutting decorative edges. Specialty snap fastening tools (12) make quick work of applying gripper snaps.

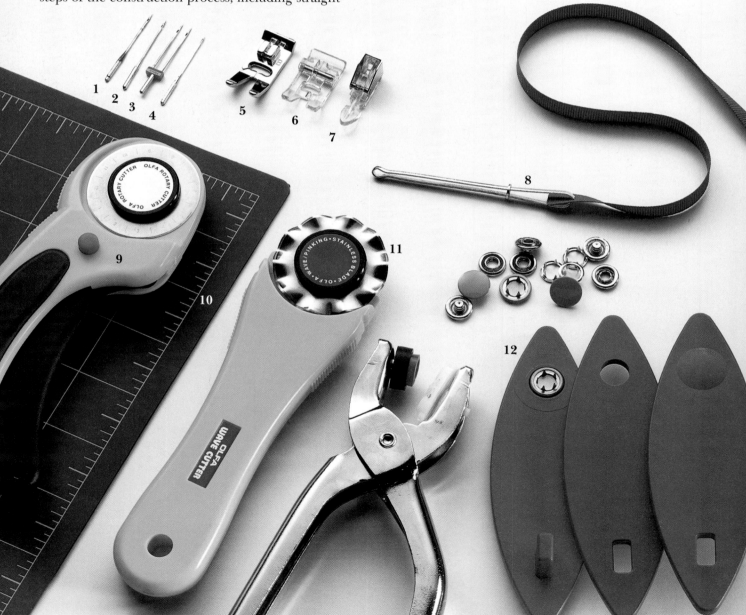

Notions

You may want to stockpile assorted notions to make it easy to vary garments made from a single pattern.

Closures on children's garments may be decorative as well as functional. Snaps come in a variety of weights and colors. Novelty buttons add a special detail, but small or shaped buttons can make it difficult for young children to dress themselves. Hook and loop tape is an easier fastener for children to manage.

Zippers may also be decorative, especially when used in contrasting colors. Zippers with fine coils are available for use on small garments. Zipper coil, with separate zipper pulls, is available in rolls of 5½ yd. (5.05 m) or by the inch (2.5 cm). It allows you to make zippers of any length and eliminates the need for keeping various sizes of zippers on hand. Dye the zipper and zipper pull to match garments or to coordinate with them.

Hardware such as D-rings, snap hooks, plastic sliders, and overall buckles can be used for suspenders, belts, and adjustable straps. Tapes and trims include ribbons, bias and twill tapes, piping, and braid. Reflective tape can be applied as a safety measure to clothing worn outdoors after dark. Appliqués add a custom look.

Getting Ready to Sew

It is important to preshrink washable fabrics, trims, and notions before laying out patterns. Preshrinking prevents the garment from shrinking, and seams and trims from puckering. It also removes excess dye and chemical finishes. Do not preshrink ribbing; this distorts the ribbing and makes accurate layout and cutting difficult.

Preshrink and dry washable fabrics as recommended in the fabric care instructions. After preshrinking 100 percent cotton fabrics, it is important to launder them several times before cutting, because cotton fabrics continue to shrink during the first several launderings. Preshrink dark and vivid cottons separately, until colors are stabilized. To preshrink fabrics that require drycleaning, steam them evenly with a steam iron and allow them to dry thoroughly on a smooth, flat surface.

Some knits, especially lightweight cotton knits, may curl and ripple after preshrinking. Remove wrinkles from the fabric before laying out the pattern, making sure the lengthwise grain is straight. Press pattern pieces with a warm, dry iron.

Plaid, striped, and checked fabrics add variety to children's garments. When using one of these fabrics, select a pattern with few pieces to make it easier to match the design. Stand back and look at the fabric to determine the dominant part of the design. The easiest way to cut these fabrics is as a single layer. Cut out each pattern piece from the fabric, and turn the cut fabric piece over to use as a pattern so the design on the second piece will match the first piece.

Tips for Laying Out Plaid Fabrics

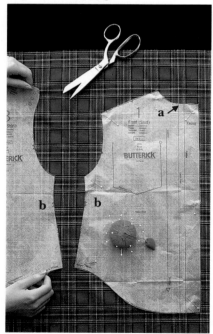

Lay out each piece in a single layer, beginning with front pattern piece. Use dominant part of design (**a**) for center front and center back. Match notches at side seams (**b**) of front and back.

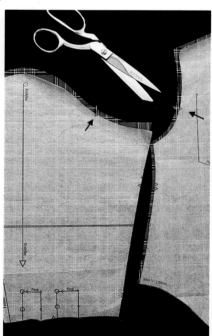

Center sleeve at same dominant part of design as center front. The design should match at the notches (arrows) of the sleeve front and armhole of garment front; notches at back may not match.

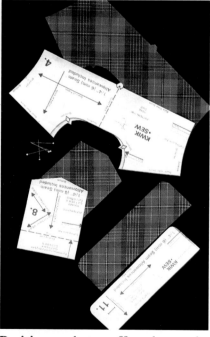

Position pockets, cuffs, yokes, and separate front bands on true bias to avoid time-consuming matching. Center a dominant design block in each pattern piece.

Tips for Layout, Cutting, and Marking

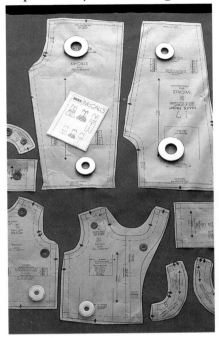

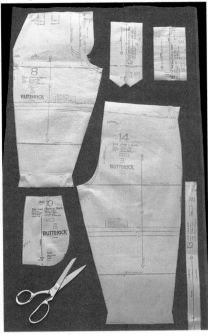

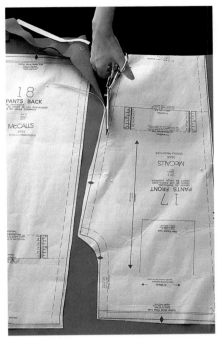

Refer to pattern layout diagram on guidesheet. Position pattern pieces, following grainline arrows and nap direction. Use weights to hold the pattern in place.

Lay out all pattern pieces on napped fabric with upper edge of pattern pieces toward same end of fabric. Corduroy and other napped fabrics wear better if sewn with the nap running down garment.

Use sharp shears and long strokes for smooth cutting. Do not trim excess pattern tissue before cutting fabric unless cutting thick fabrics such as corduroy and quilted fabric.

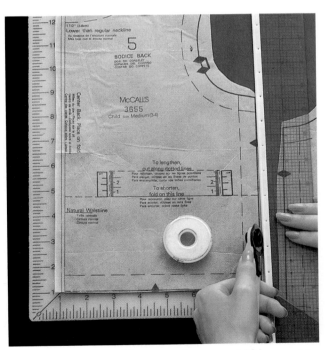

Use rotary cutter with protective mat, shifting mat to cut other pieces. Use metal-edged ruler for straight edges, placing blade side of rotary cutter next to ruler; trim off notches. Small rotary cutter may be used for tight curves or complex shapes.

Transfer all pattern markings after cutting. Make short clip no more than ⅛" (3 mm) into seam allowance to mark notches, dots, center front, center back, and ends of darts and pleats. To mark pockets, pin through pattern and fabric, lift pattern, and mark each fabric layer with chalk or washable marking pen.

Hems & Seams

Topstitched hems and seams can be decorative as well as functional. Use a matching or contrasting color thread that coordinates with other items of clothing.

Machine-stitched hems are fast and durable, and are a good alternative for ribbing at cuffs, waistlines, and pants legs on children's clothing.

Select seams and seam finishes based on the type of fabric. Also consider if the seam will show through the garment, if strength is required at the seam, and if the seam will be comfortable when it is next to the skin.

Hems. Topstitched hem (**1**) has one or more rows of topstitching near upper edge of a finished hem allowance. Blindstitch (**2**) by machine for a hem that is nearly invisible from the right side. The cover stitch (**3**), available on some sergers, is a popular hem on ready-to-wear clothes. Stitch from the right side or the wrong side, depending on the look preferred. Stitch about ¼" (6 mm) below cut edge of hem allowance and trim close to stitching. For a narrow hem (**4**), trim hem allowance to ½" (1.3 cm); press to wrong side. Open hem, and fold raw edge to hemline crease. Fold again to make double-fold hem; topstitch one or two rows as desired. Use a rolled hem (**5**), sewn on a serger, for lightweight or sheer fabrics. Stitch with right side up; fabric rolls under to the wrong side. A twin-needle topstitched hem (**6**) is suitable for knits, because the bobbin thread zigzags on the wrong side and allows stitches to stretch.

Seams and seam finishes. For plain seams, press open ⅝" (1.5 cm) seam allowances. Finish edges with overlock stitching (**1**) sewn on a serger, or with a three-step zigzag (**2**). A French seam (**3**) is neat and inconspicuous from the right side, but it is difficult to use on curves. For ¼" (6 mm) seam allowances on stretch fabrics, use an overedge stitch (**4**) or a narrow zigzag stitch (**5**); stretch seams slightly while stitching. Press narrow seams to one side.

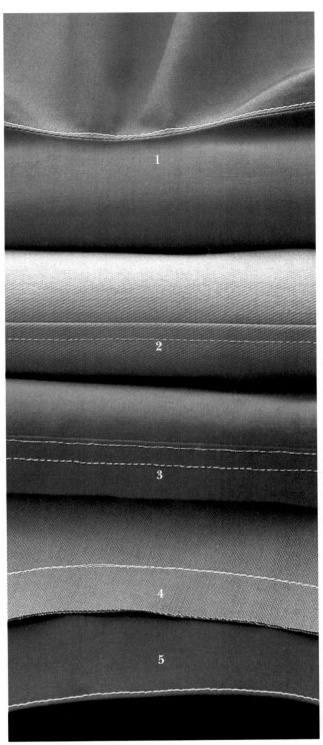

Reinforced seams. Understitched seam (**1**) stabilizes the seam by stitching seam allowances to the facing. Welt seam (**2**) has seam allowances pressed to one side and topstitched to garment. Mock flat-fell seam (**3**) has exposed seam allowances on the wrong side of the garment with topstitching and edgestitching. Double-stitching (**4**) is stitching sewn over previous stitching. Edgestitching (**5**) is stitching sewn on the right side of the garment, through both seam allowances, as close to the seamline as possible.

Overlock seams. 3-thread stitch (**1**) stretches with the fabric and can be used as a seam or edge finish, but it is not recommended for woven fabrics in areas of stress. 4-thread safety stitch (**2**) is strong and stable for woven fabrics, but it does not stretch on knit seams. 4-thread mock safety stitch (**3**) provides an additional line of stitching, has stretch, and can be used on knit fabrics.

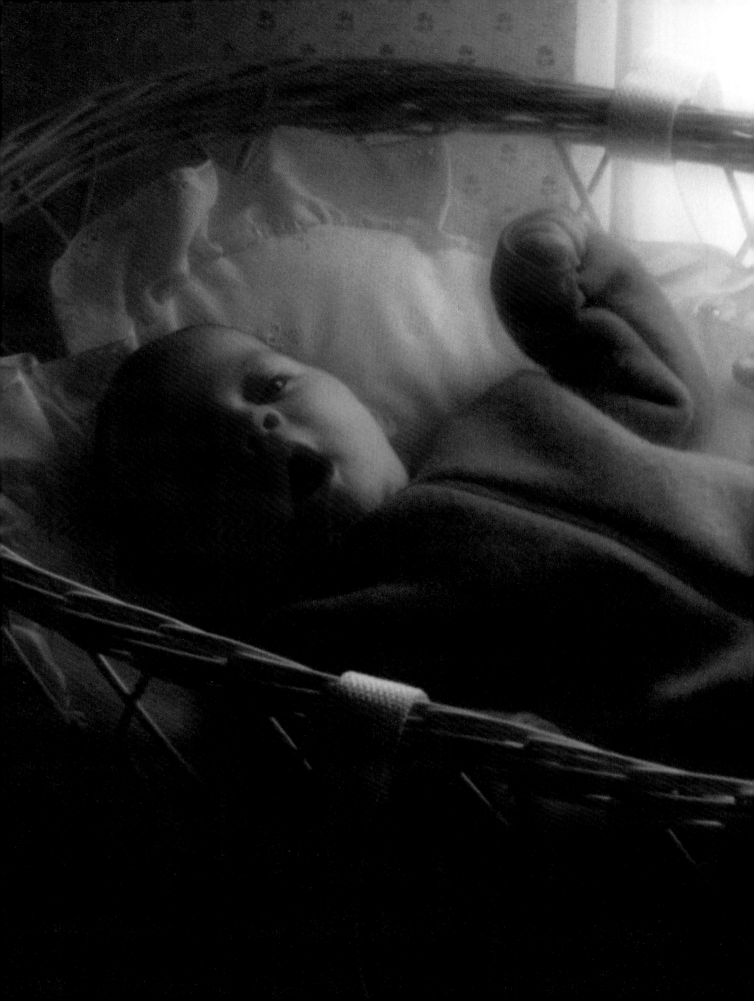

Infants

Sewing a Basic Layette

Many of the items in a basic layette, such as receiving blankets, hooded towels, bibs, kimonos, and buntings, are easy and practical to sew. Multi-sized layette patterns are available for making most of these items. For everyday wear, use simple, loose-fitting designs and high-quality fabrics that are easy to sew and launder.

Cotton or cotton-blend fabrics are good choices because cotton breathes, absorbs moisture, and is easy to launder. Infants are most comfortable in soft fabrics.

Stretch knits adapt well to movement, growth, and easy dressing. Woven fabrics such as flannel, seersucker, and broadcloth work well with the addition of ribbing at the neck, sleeves, and hem.

Federal regulations require that garments designed for children's sleepwear meet flame-retardancy standards. Look for this information on the ends of fabric bolts. Cotton must be blended with synthetic fibers to accept this treatment.

If you select basic styles, you can use timesaving techniques that allow you to sew several garments in a short time. By choosing high-quality fabrics, you

can sew garments superior to the average ready-to-wear items, and often at a more reasonable cost.

Receiving blankets and hooded towels are important to a layette. Several blankets or towels can be made at a time. Hooded towels can also be used as beach towels.

Bibs can easily be made by sewing ribbing and a neck closure to a hand towel. Older infants and toddlers enjoy large bibs with sleeves and pockets, which you can coordinate with several garments.

Kimonos of soft flannel or knits are comfortable for an infant during the first several months, and the open lower edge of the kimono allows for easy diapering. If the neck and armhole openings are large enough, the garment can also be used as a dress or T-shirt in later months. Buntings, adaptations of the kimono,

are closed at the lower edge for outerwear use and are often made of quilted fabrics, double-faced polyester bunting, or other soft, heavyweight fabrics.

Infant Accessories

Patterns are available for infant seat covers, pillows, diaper stackers, high chair pads, and other accessories. All of these can be customized by using coordinating colors, extra padding, warm fabrics, ruffles, and piping. Patterns may need to be adapted to the specific needs of the equipment; for example, tie and strap locations may need to be adjusted.

Receiving Blankets & Hooded Towels

Receiving blankets and hooded towels can be made large enough to accommodate the growth of the child. Choose soft, warm, and absorbent woven or knit fabrics. Select from flannel, interlock, jersey, thermal knit, terry cloth and stretch terry. Two layers of lightweight fabric can be used with wrong sides together. Round all corners for easy edge application.

Cut a 36" (91.5 cm) square blanket or towel from 1 yd. (.95 m) of 45" or 60" (115 or 152.5 cm) wide fabric. When using 45" (115 cm) wide fabric, the mock binding and hood require an additional ¼ yd. (.25 m). Cut a 1½" (3.8 cm) wide binding strip on the lengthwise or crosswise grain, 2" (5 cm) longer than the distance around the item; piece, as necessary. Press binding in half, with wrong sides together.

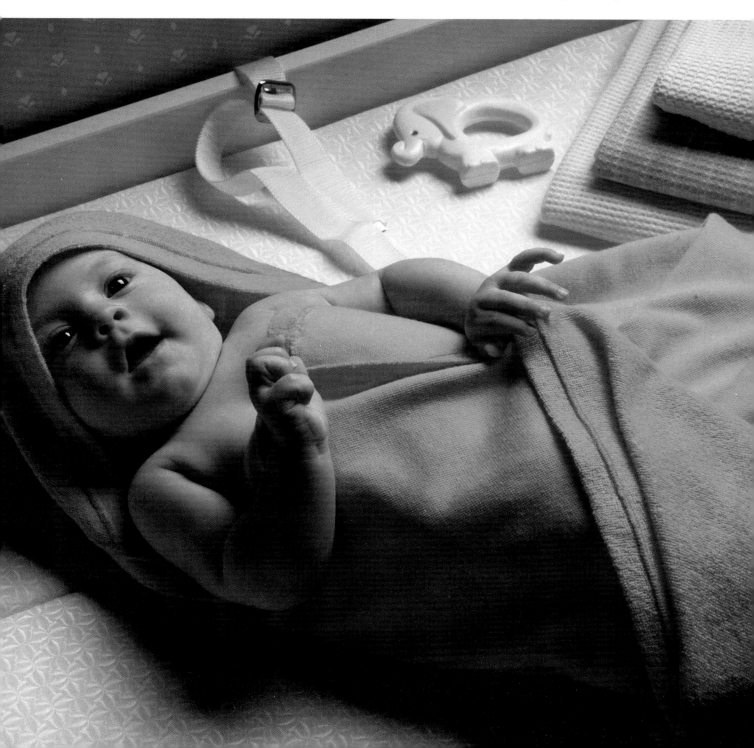

How to Finish Edges with a Mock Binding

  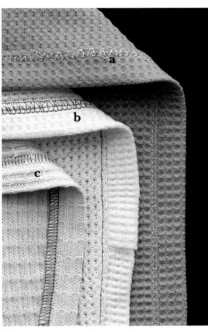

1) Use overedge stitch or serge binding to right side of fabric, starting 1½" (3.8 cm) from end of binding. Stitch to within 2" (5 cm) of start of binding, stretching fabric slightly at corners; do not stretch binding. (If flatlock stitch on serger is used, stitch *wrong* sides together.)

2) Fold 1" (2.5 cm) of binding to inside; lap around first end of binding. Continue stitching binding to fabric, stitching over previous stitches for 1" (2.5 cm) to secure the ends.

3) Turn seam allowance toward blanket or towel; topstitch through all layers of overedged **(a)** or serged **(b)** seam, to hold seam allowances flat. If flatlock **(c)** stitch is used, pull binding and fabric flat.

How to Sew a Hooded Towel

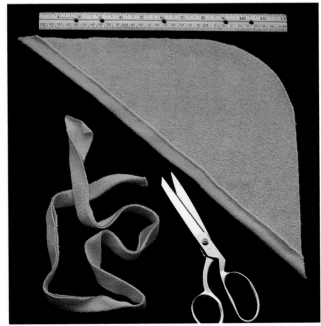 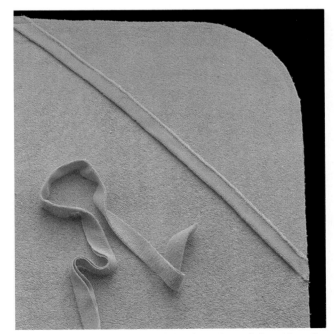

1) Cut a right triangle with two 12" (30.5 cm) sides from matching or contrasting fabric. Round right angle corner, and finish diagonal edge with mock binding, above.

2) Position wrong side of the hood to right side of the towel. Stitch triangle to one rounded corner of towel, ¼" (6 mm) from matched edges. Finish outside edges, above.

Bibs

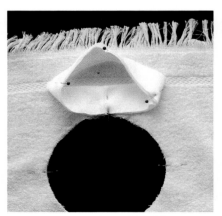

Infant bibs are quick and easy to make. Create durable bibs from terry cloth or knit fabric or from fingertip towels, and customize the bibs with simple appliqué techniques and bias tape. Increase absorbency by using a double layer of fabric. Back a fabric bib with soft, pliable plastic to protect clothing; finish edges with wide double-fold bias tape. Or use a fingertip towel with prefinished edges.

Custom Bibs

Attach a toy or pacifier to a bib with a snap-on strip **(1)**. Stitch together the edges of a 12" (30.5 cm) strip of wide double-fold bias tape, and fold under the ends of the strip. Attach one end to the bib with the ball half of a gripper snap. Attach the socket half of the gripper snap to the other end of the tape. Slip the toy or pacifier onto the tape; snap securely to the bib.

A purchased squeaker can be inserted between the appliqué and bib **(2)** before you stitch the appliqué (page 95).

A fingertip towel makes an absorbent, washable bib. Fold the towel for double absorbency under the chin **(3)**, and attach double-fold bias tape around the neck edge.

How to Make a Pullover Bib

1) Use fingertip towel. Cut 5" (12.5 cm) circle with center of circle one-third the distance from one end of towel. Cut 3" (7.5 cm) wide ribbing, with length two-thirds the circumference. Stitch short ends to form circle, using ¼" (6 mm) seam allowance.

2) Fold ribbing in half, with wrong sides together. Divide ribbing and neck edge into fourths; pin-mark. Matching pins, and with seam at center back, pin ribbing to neck edge, with raw edges even. Stitch ¼" (6 mm) seam, stretching ribbing to fit neckline.

3) Fold seam allowance toward bib. Edgestitch to bib through all layers.

How to Make a Tie-on Bib

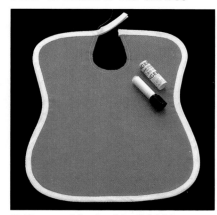

1) Press wide double-fold bias tape to follow curve of outer edge of bib. Glue-baste tape over raw edge of bib, positioning the wider tape edge on the wrong side; edgestitch in place.

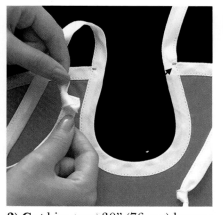

2) Cut bias tape 30" (76 cm) longer than neck curve. Center bias tape over the neck edge; glue-baste. Edgestitch from one end of tie around neckline to other end. Bar tack bias tape at edge of bib (arrow) by zigzagging in place; tie knot at each end.

Alternative. Cut fingertip towel as for pullover bib, opposite. Fold so neck opening forms a half circle. Zigzag raw edges together with wide stitch. Apply bias tape for ties and neck finish, step 2, left.

Kimonos

Timesaving techniques enable you to cut and sew several kimonos at one time. Neckline openings for woven fabrics should be at least 1" to 2" (2.5 to 5 cm) larger than the infant's head. Openings for knit fabrics do not need to be as large, because knits will stretch to fit over the head.

Use the flat method of construction to sew infant-size garments; complete as much stitching as possible while the garment is flat. Access to parts of tiny garments becomes difficult once seams are completed. Apply all ribbing while one seam is still open.

How to Sew a Kimono with Ribbing (flat method)

1) **Measure** and cut ribbing for neck, wrists, and lower edge (page 17); fold in half lengthwise. Straight-stitch or serge garment front and back together at one shoulder seam, right sides together.

2) **Divide** ribbing and neck edge into fourths; pin-mark. Pin the ribbing and the neck edge together at marks and ends. Overedge stitch or serge ¼" (6 mm) seam, stretching ribbing to fit neck edge as you sew.

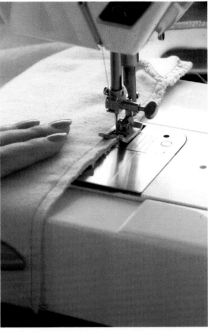

3) **Straight-stitch** or serge other shoulder seam, right sides together; carefully match ribbing edge and ribbing seam. Finish the seam allowances, if necessary.

4) **Divide** ribbing and wrist edge in half; pin-mark. Pin and stitch as in step 2, above.

5) **Straight-stitch** or serge one underarm seam, with right sides together; carefully match ribbing edge and ribbing seam. Finish seam allowances, if necessary.

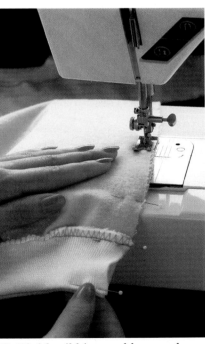

6) **Divide** ribbing and lower edge; pin and stitch as in step 2, above. Stitch remaining underarm seam as in step 5, left. Finish seam allowances, if necessary.

Customizing Kimonos

To add a placket, slash the front of the kimono and apply a continuous self-binding. Position the opening off-center so fasteners line up on the center front.

For a boy's garment, mark the placket opening to the right of center to lap left over right. For a girl's garment, mark the placket opening to the left of center to lap right over left. The photos that follow are for a girl's kimono. Mark a 6" (15 cm) opening 3/8" (1 cm) from the center front for a 3/4" (2 cm) finished placket width. Cut a binding strip 12" × 2" (30.5 × 5 cm) on the lengthwise grain. Press the binding strip in half lengthwise, wrong sides together. Open the strip, and press under 1/4" (6 mm) on one long edge.

For a kimono pattern without a cuff, add sleeve mitts to be folded over the baby's hands. Finish the kimono with a mandarin collar and gripper snaps.

How to Apply a Continuous Self-bound Placket

1) Mark the placket opening, and cut binding, above. Staystitch 1/4" (6 mm) from marked line, tapering to a point. Shorten stitches for 1/2" (1.3 cm) on each side of point, and take one short stitch at point. Slash along line to, but not through, point.

2) Hold placket opening straight; pin to unpressed edge of binding, right sides together. Stitch over staystitching with 1/4" (6 mm) seam allowance on binding; raw edges match only at seam ends. Add sleeve mitts, opposite. Stitch shoulder seams. Add collar, opposite.

3) Place pressed edge of binding on seamline of overlap, *wrong* sides together; pin. For underlap, place pressed edge on seamline, *right* sides together; pin. Stitch overlap and underlap at neckline.

4) Fold the binding to inside of the garment, with fold on the seamline. Edgestitch binding over previous stitching; stitch to within 1" (2.5 cm) of neckline.

5) Pin overlap binding flat to inside of garment. Mark topstitching line on front side of overlap near the inside fold.

6) Topstitch through garment and binding, beginning at lower end of overlap (arrow); pivot at marked line, and stitch to neckline. Pivot; edgestitch around neckline through the garment and seam allowances, stretching slightly. Apply gripper snap at top of placket.

How to Attach a Mandarin Collar

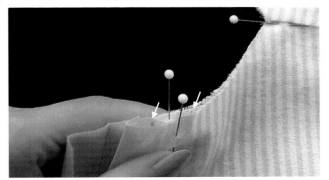

1) Cut ribbing for collar 2" (5 cm) wide and 2" (5 cm) shorter than neck opening. Fold in half lengthwise. Mark center back. Apply placket as in steps 1 and 2, opposite. Fold front, matching shoulder seams; pin halfway between placket seams (arrows) to mark adjusted center fronts.

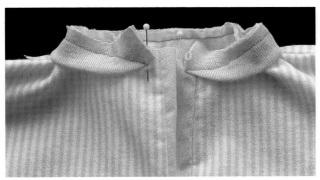

2) Pin collar to neck edge at center back, with right sides together and raw edges even. Place pin on folded edge of collar ¼" (6 mm) from each short end. Match pins to center fronts; pin securely. Stitch collar to neck edge, stretching collar to fit. Trim collar to match neck edge. Complete placket, steps 3 to 6, opposite.

How to Add Sleeve Mitts

1) Cut ribbing for sleeve mitt 6" (15 cm) long on lengthwise grain and 1" (2.5 cm) wider than width of sleeve. Fold ribbing in half crosswise to 3" (7.5 cm), and lay under end of sleeve. Trim to match shape of sleeve. Stitch folded ribbing to wrong side of sleeve back at lower edge, using ¼" (6 mm) seam and matching raw edges. Turn mitt to right side.

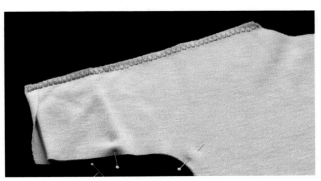

2) Pin kimono front to back at shoulder and underarm seams, right sides together. Fold hem allowance of sleeve front over finished sleeve back. Stitch shoulder and underarm seams.

3) Turn back hem allowance of sleeve front, encasing seam allowances. (Do not turn garment right side out.) Topstitch hem, stitching through sleeve back and mitt; use twin needle, if desired.

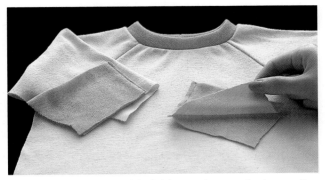

One-piece sleeve. Fold ribbing as in step 1, above. Cut mitt one-half the width of sleeve plus ¼" (6 mm). Stitch ¼" (6 mm) seam in one short end; turn seam to inside. Lay mitt on right side of back of sleeve, with seam at center; edgestitch short end at center. Stitch underarm seam. Turn hem allowance to wrong side. Topstitch hem as in step 3, left.

Buntings

Patterns are available for making baby buntings with all the features of ready-to-wear. They may have hoods for cold-weather use or simple ribbed neckline edges for everyday sleeping comfort. Some styles have a gusset at the bottom for growing room. Others may have split-leg styling for convenience when riding in a car seat.

Because most buntings are made of knit fabrics or synthetic fleece, the most difficult part of the bunting construction is inserting the zipper. However, Totally Stable®, a convenient iron-on tear-away stabilizer, makes zipper insertion easy. Purchase an 18" or 20" (46 or 51 cm) zipper, or cut the desired length from continuous zipper coil (page 19).

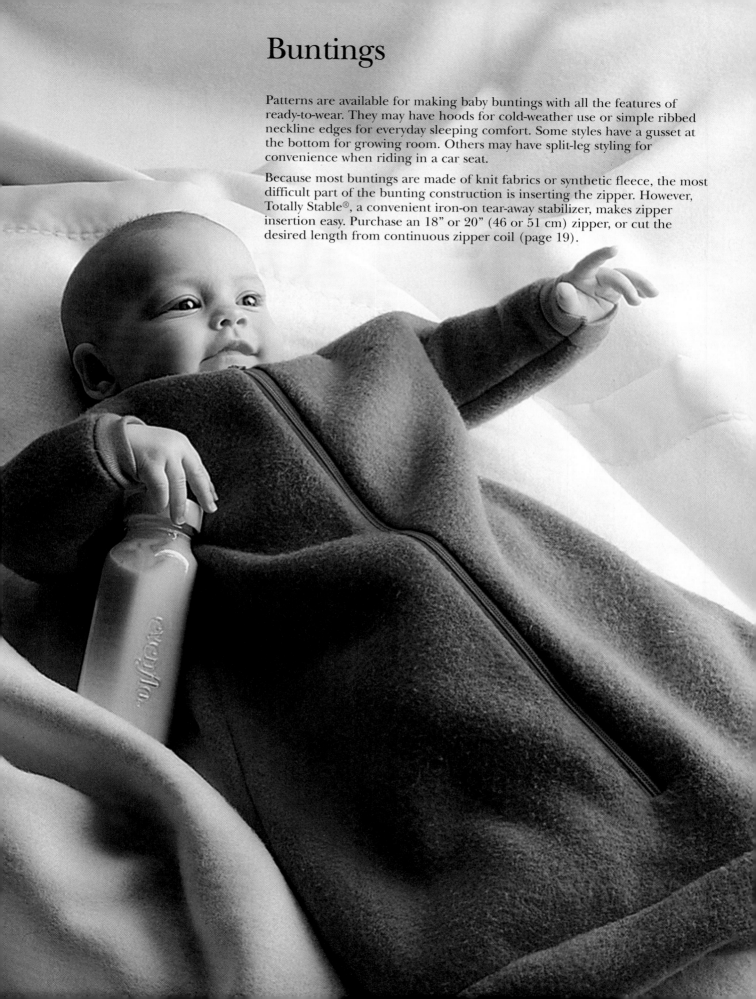

How to Insert a Zipper in a Bunting

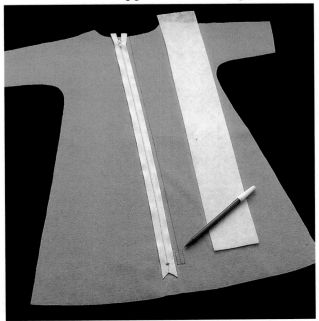

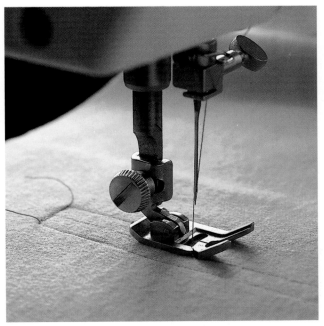

1) Mark line for zipper opening at center front from neck edge to zipper stop. Draw stitching box across lower end of line and ¼" (6 mm) on each side of line. Cut iron-on tear-away stabilizer 3" (7.5 cm) wide and 2" (5 cm) longer than zipper opening; iron onto wrong side of fabric under line for opening.

2) Staystitch across bottom line of stitching box; pivot at corner, and stitch to neck edge ¼" (6 mm) from marked line, using about 15 stitches per inch (2.5 cm). Repeat on other side of line, beginning at bottom line of stitching box.

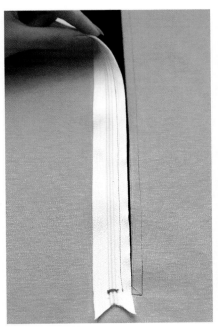

3) Slash center line carefully to ¼" (6 mm) from bottom line; clip diagonally to, but not through, the lower corners.

4) Place one edge of zipper along edge of opening, right sides together, with zipper stop at bottom line of stitching box. With *garment side up*, stitch over previous stitching from zipper stop to neck edge, using zipper foot. Repeat for other edge, stitching from bottom to top.

5) Fold lower part of garment and stabilizer back at bottom of zipper, exposing the triangle of the stitching box and the end of the zipper tape. Double-stitch across triangle on the staystitching to secure triangle to zipper. Remove stabilizer.

Wardrobe Planning

Plan a child's wardrobe before you begin to sew. If the garments you sew are coordinated, they are more versatile and will have a different look with each ensemble. The child can easily select garments to wear together. Planning a wardrobe does not mean, however, that all garments must be made at one time.

Begin wardrobe planning by considering colors. Notice which colors are in style in ready-to-wear garments and which colors the child likes. Many garments and colors are suitable for either sex, so large portions of a wardrobe can be used by boys and girls.

Decide which colors will be central to the wardrobe. For basic wardrobe items, select colors and fabrics that can be worn year-round. Take swatches of fabrics with you when you shop. Garments for children do not take large amounts of fabric, so stockpile remnants in the wardrobe colors. You may want to purchase trims in coordinating colors for future use.

Wardrobe Basics

The core garments of a child's wardrobe include shirts, pants, overalls, a jacket, and for girls, a skirt and jumper. For sewing these core items, you may want to select a simple pattern that contains directions for sewing several garments, and vary the fabrics, trims, and finishes.

You can use one basic pants pattern for sweatpants, jeans with rolled cuffs, shorts, and pants with a mock fly. From a T-shirt pattern, you can make a shirt with a rugby placket and a pullover shirt with a kangaroo pocket. From one skirt pattern, make a skirt with a mock fly and another with a ribbing waistband. A simple yoked dress can be a school dress or a party dress, depending on the fabric.

Personalizing

To personalize simple pattern shapes, use coordinating fabrics for color blocking. Mix woven fabrics with knits. Sew the body of a shirt with a neck placket from a woven fabric, and the sleeves from a knit. Use piping to highlight the neckline, armholes, side seams, or pocket seams. Repeat trims, such as appliqués or buttons on shirts, to coordinate with pants or skirts.

Adding Durability

Build in durability as you construct children's garments. Seams and knees are subject to the most stress during dressing and active play, but both areas can be strengthened easily as you sew the garment.

Seams are most vulnerable at the crotch, shoulder, neck, and armhole. Strengthen the crotch and armhole seams with double-stitched, mock flat-fell, or edgestitched seams. Reinforce shoulder and neckline seams with decorative twin-needle topstitching, stitching before crossing with another seam. Machine-stitch hems for added strength in activewear (page 22).

The knee area wears out faster than any other part of a child's garment and is difficult to reach for repairs. Flat construction techniques allow you to reinforce knee areas as you construct the garment.

Patches

Tightly woven fabrics make the most durable patches. Interface, pad, or quilt patches for extra durability and protection at the knee, especially for crawling toddlers. Fuse the patch to the garment to make the application easier and to strengthen the patch.

Decorative knee patches are cut according to the child's size. For infants, cut the patch 3½" × 4" (9 × 10 cm); for toddlers, 3¾" × 5" (9.5 × 12.5 cm); for children, 4½" × 6" (11.5 × 15 cm).

Round the corners of decorative patches to simplify application and to eliminate sharp corners that could catch and tear.

How to Add Decorative Knee Patches

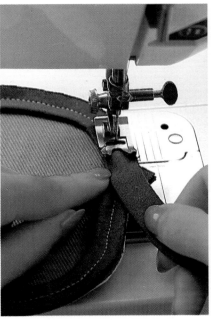

1) Cut two patches to size (opposite); round corners. Iron paper-backed fusible web to back of patches. Cut two strips of fabric for piping (1" × 24" (2.5 × 61 cm); cut on bias for woven fabrics or crosswise grain for knits.

2) Press strips in half lengthwise, wrong sides together. Stitch to right side of each patch, raw edges even, with ¼" (6 mm) seam allowance.

3) Curve ends of piping into seam allowance, so folded ends overlap and taper to raw edge. Trim piping even with raw edge of patch.

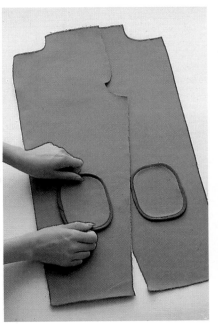

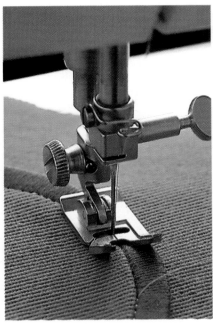

4) Trim seam allowance to ⅛" (3 mm). Press seam allowance to wrong side of patch, pulling piping out from patch. Remove paper backing from fusible web.

5) Fuse one patch to front of pants leg, parallel to hemline with center of patch slightly below center of knee. On the other pants leg, align second patch with first; fuse.

6) Stitch patch to garment, stitching in the ditch. Finish pants according to pattern directions.

Adding Grow Room

Build in grow room when you construct children's clothing, to get the maximum amount of wear from the garments. Without this extra room, a child going through a rapid growth spurt may be unable to wear a garment that is well liked and in good condition. The easiest place to add grow room is at the lower edge or sleeve hem. Rolled-up lined cuffs can be gradually lowered as the child grows. To add a coordinated look, select a lining fabric to match a shirt or other part of the ensemble. Cut lining on the straight grain or bias; add interest with a plaid or stripe. When sewing a garment that has straps, add extra length to the straps, and use overall buckles for easy length adjustment.

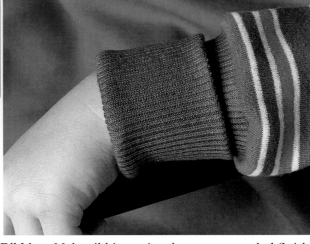

Ribbing. Make ribbing twice the recommended finish width. Fold the ribbing up, and gradually unroll it to add length as the child grows. Add ribbing to outgrown sleeves or pants legs by opening the hem and using the hemline for the new stitching line.

Inserts and trims (opposite). Planning carefully for balanced finished proportions, cut off the lower edge of the garment. Cut an insert of coordinating fabric, lace, or eyelet 1" (2.5 cm) wider than desired length, to allow for 1/4" (6 mm) seam allowances on insert and garment. Stitch upper edge of insert to garment, then stitch lower section of garment to insert. Trims with finished edges can be stitched to the right or wrong side of a garment at the hemline for added length.

How to Add Lined Cuffs

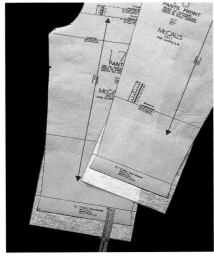

1) Adjust pattern at hem; lengthen hem allowance to 2½" (6.5 cm). Straighten side seams above original hemline for 4" (10 cm) to eliminate taper. Cut out garment; assemble according to pattern directions, but do not hem.

2) Cut two cuffs 3½" (9 cm) wide, and 1" (2.5 cm) longer than the circumference of finished sleeve or pants leg. Stitch short ends of cuff, right sides together, using ½" (1.3 cm) seam; press open. Serge upper edge, or turn under 1/4" (6 mm), and press.

3) Stitch cuff to garment, with right sides together and raw edges even, using 1/4" (6 mm) seam; match cuff seam to inseam. Turn cuff at stitching line, and press to wrong side of garment; topstitch at lower and upper edges. Fold cuff to right side.

Shirts

For a versatile shirt pattern, choose a loose-fitting, basic T-shirt style with a round neck. Using one pattern, you can make several shirts by varying the design with different neck, cuff, and hem finishes.

Fabric choices also add variety. Most loose-fitting T-shirt patterns may be sewn from lightweight knits and wovens for warm weather. Sweatshirt fleece or flannel make a warm shirt for cooler weather.

For easier sewing of a child's shirt, you may want to change the sewing sequence from the usual pattern directions. Do as much stitching as possible while the garment is flat. Pockets and appliqués are easier to apply before any seams are stitched. The flat method of ribbing application (page 33) is easier on Toddlers'

sizes, which have small neck and arm openings. The tubular ribbing application (page 48) is neater and may be preferred for Children's sizes.

Prefinished collars, cuffs, and waistbands are sold separately or in sets. They have a prefinished outer edge for a ready-to-wear look and are available in solid colors or in a variety of stripes and edge finishes. Prefinished collars, cuffs, and waistbands should be 1" to 3" (2.5 to 7.5 cm) smaller than the opening. If an appropriate child's size is unavailable, trim an adult size to fit. Use a prefinished collar for a T-shirt or for a shirt with a convertible collar. Use prefinished cuffs to finish a ribbed-top pocket.

How to Apply Prefinished Collar, Cuffs, and Waistband

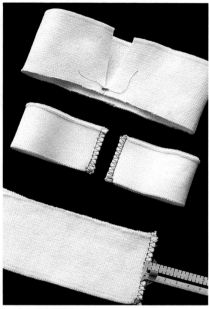

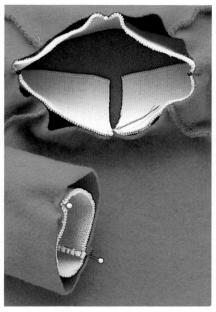

1) Trim short ends so collar, cuffs, and waistband are 1" to 3" (2.5 to 7.5 cm) shorter than garment edge; on collars, trim an equal amount from each end. Trim the width, if desired. Apply liquid fray preventer to short ends of collar.

2) Butt collar ends, and join with bar tack by zigzagging in place just inside neck seamline. Join short ends of cuff and waistband, using ¼" (6 mm) seam.

3) Divide collar, waistband, and garment edges into fourths; divide cuffs and sleeves in half. Place collar ends at center front, cuff seams at sleeve seams, and waistband seam at side seam. Attach as for ribbing, steps 2 and 3, page 48.

How to Apply a Prefinished Collar and Ribbing

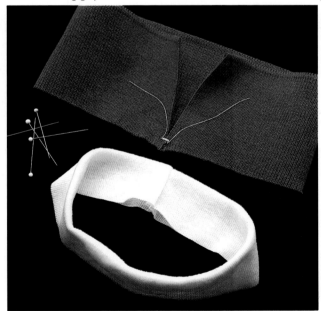

1) Trim prefinished collar, if necessary, as in step 1, above. Butt ends, and join with bar tack by zigzagging in place just inside neck seamline. Cut ribbing for narrow crew neck (page 17). Join ends, using ¼" (6 mm) seam; fold in half lengthwise, wrong sides together. Divide collar, ribbing, and neck edge into fourths; pin-mark.

2) Pin ribbing to right side of garment at neck edge, with pin marks matching and raw edges even; position ribbing seam at back seam of raglan sleeve, at shoulder seam, or at center back. Pin collar over ribbing, with raw edges even. Place collar ends at center front. Stitch, stretching ribbing and collar to fit neck edge as in step 3, page 48.

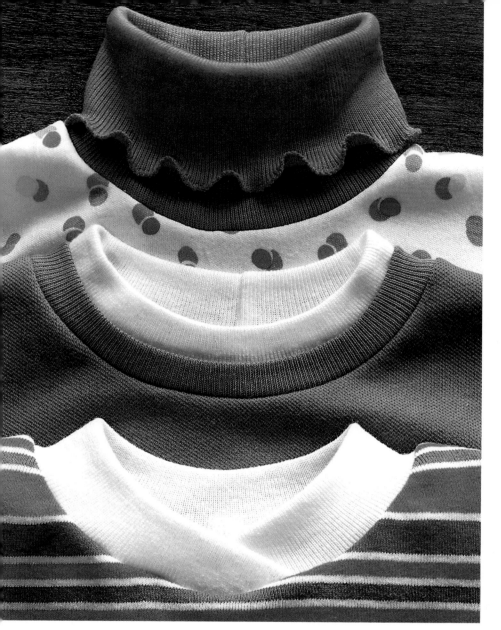

Ribbed Edges

Ribbing makes an attractive finish for necklines, cuffs, or waistlines on either knit or woven fabric. When using ribbing to finish a shirt made from woven fabric, check the size of the neck opening on the pattern to be sure the garment will fit over the child's head. Neck openings should be 1" to 2" (2.5 to 5 cm) larger than the child's head. It may be necessary to enlarge the opening or use a larger size pattern.

Ribbing does not have a right or a wrong side, so it can be folded with either side up. It can be applied using the flat method (page 33) or the tubular method, below. You can use the tubular method with large openings to produce a neater finish, because the seam that joins the ribbing into a circle is enclosed. Place the ribbing seam where it will be least visible.

For a double ribbing neck finish, combine two ribbings of different widths. For a lapped ribbing, cut a standard crew neck width, and lap the ends instead of joining them into a circle.

Lettuce edging can be used to finish the edge of the ribbing or knit fabric for a feminine look. Match the color of the thread to the fabric, or use a coordinating color thread.

How to Apply Ribbing Using the Tubular Method

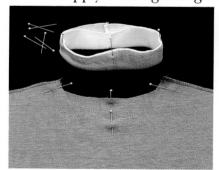

1) Cut ribbing two-thirds the length of neck opening; cut the width for standard crew neck (page 17). Join ribbing ends with ¼" (6 mm) seam. Fold the ribbing in half lengthwise. Divide ribbing and garment edges into fourths; pin-mark.

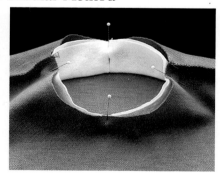

2) Position ribbing seam at center back or shoulder seam; pin ribbing to right side of garment, with raw edges even, matching pins.

3) Serge or use an overedge stitch (page 22) to apply ribbing to the garment, using ¼" (6 mm) seam; ribbing is on top and raw edges are even. Stretch ribbing between pins to fit garment.

How to Apply Double Ribbing

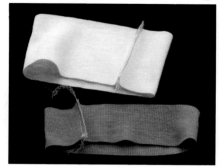

1) Cut two pieces of ribbing two-thirds the length of neck opening; cut one ribbing width for standard crew neck, and the other ribbing width for a narrow crew neck (page 17). Join short ends of each ribbing with ¼" (6 mm) seam.

2) Fold each piece of ribbing in half lengthwise, with wrong sides together. Pin narrow ribbing over wide ribbing, with raw edges even and seams matching. Divide ribbing and garment edges into fourths, and pin-mark.

3) Position ribbing seams at center back or shoulder seam. Pin ribbings to right side of garment, matching pins, with wide ribbing on top and raw edges even. Stitch as for tubular method, step 3, opposite.

How to Apply Lapped Ribbing

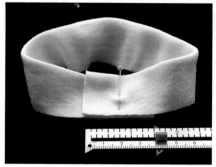

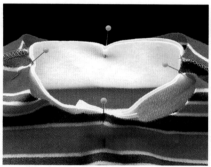

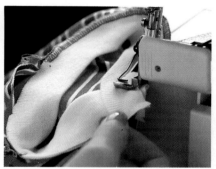

1) Cut ribbing two-thirds the length of neck opening plus 1½" (3.8 cm); cut width for standard crew neck (page 17). Fold in half lengthwise. Lap ends ¾" (2 cm); mark center of overlap with pin.

2) Divide ribbing and garment into fourths; pin-mark. Pin ribbing to right side of garment, with center of overlap at center front and raw edges even, matching pins.

3) Curve ends of ribbing into seam allowance, so folded ends overlap and taper to raw edges. Stitch as for tubular method, step 3, opposite, starting at center back.

How to Finish Ribbing and Knits with Lettuce Edging

Conventional method. Zigzag closely spaced stitches over ribbing fold or folded edge of hem, placing fold at center of presser foot and stretching the fabric as you stitch. The more you stretch the fabric, the more ruffled the edge will be. For hems, trim the hem allowance close to stitching.

Serged method. Adjust serger for rolled hem setting according to manufacturer's directions. Stitch along ribbing fold or folded edge of hem, stretching fabric as you stitch. Do not cut the folded edge with the serger knives. The more you stretch the fabric, the more ruffled the edge will be. For hems, trim hem allowance close to stitching.

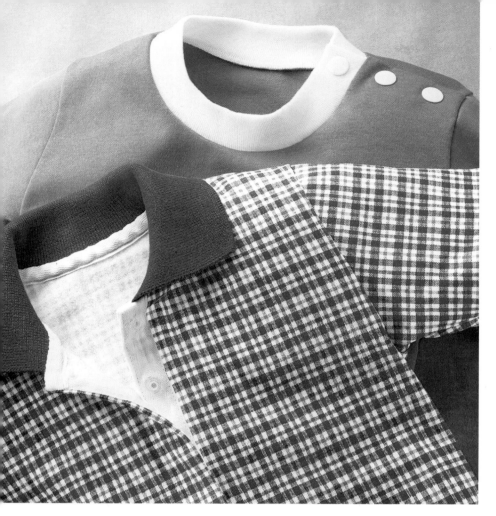

Snap Closures

Snap closures at the neckline allow more room for the head and make easy dressing for young fingers. Choose one of two methods, depending on the style of the shirt. Convert a left shoulder seam on a ribbed neckline to a snap opening, using individual gripper snaps. Or sew a front opening on a knit or woven shirt with a collar, using snap tape.

Gripper snaps are available in many decorative styles and colors, and are easy to apply with special tools. Since snap tape iș available in limited colors, check the selection before deciding on the shirt fabric. Stitch snap tape carefully to maintain alignment of the fabric design. For a neat look when the placket is open, finish the neck edges with twill tape or bias binding. Always preshrink fabric and tapes before constructing the shirt.

How to Apply Gripper Snaps to a Shoulder Opening

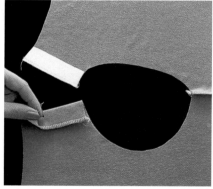

1) **Cut** out shirt pieces, allowing 1" (2.5 cm) seam allowances on left front and back shoulders. Cut two strips of fusible interfacing 1" (2.5 cm) wide and length of shoulder seam; fuse to underside of left shoulder seam allowances. Finish raw edges; fold left front seam allowance under 1" (2.5 cm), and press. Lap over left back shoulder seam allowance; baste within armhole seam allowance. Stitch right shoulder seam.

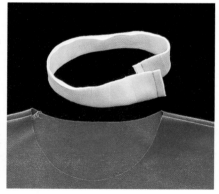

2) **Cut** ribbing 1½" (3.8 cm) longer than pattern. Cut two 1¼" (3.2 cm) pieces of fusible interfacing half the width of ribbing; fuse to underside of ribbing ends. Fold ribbing in half lengthwise, right sides together; stitch ¼" (6 mm) seams at short ends. Turn and press. Mark 1" (2.5 cm) from one end of ribbing.

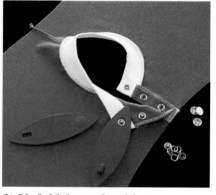

3) **Unfold** front shoulder seam. Divide neckline into fourths, beginning at foldline; pin-mark. Repeat for ribbing, beginning at mark. Pin ribbing to right side of neck edge, matching marks; stitch as on page 48, step 3. Turn shoulder seam allowance back over ribbing; straight-stitch across end ¼" (6 mm) from neck edge. Refold seam allowance to inside. Apply gripper snaps, following manufacturer's directions; place one on ribbing and two on shoulder. Complete garment.

How to Apply Snap Tape to a Full-length Shirt Opening

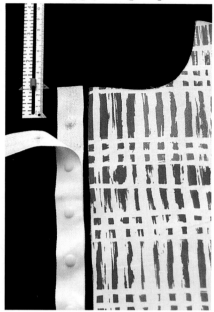

1) Cut the snap tape the length of the opening, with top and bottom snaps about 1" (2.5 cm) from raw edges. Press narrow double-fold hem to wrong side.

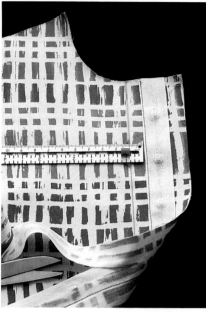

2) Mark center front on *right* side of *overlap*. Glue-baste tape to facing, with ball side up and tape edge ⅜" (1 cm) from center front. Edgestitch edge nearest center front, using zipper foot; at lower edge, turn under tape to match pressed hem. Trim facing to ¼" (6 mm).

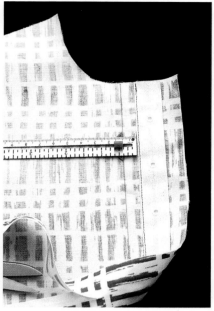

3) Mark center front on *wrong* side of underlap. Glue-baste tape to facing, with socket side up and edge ⅜" (1 cm) from center front. Edgestitch edge nearest center front, using zipper foot; at lower edge, turn under tape to match pressed hem. Trim facing to ¼" (6 mm).

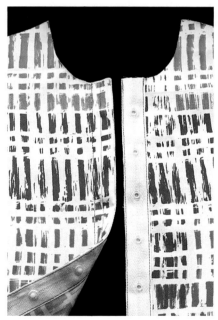

4) Turn ball side of tape to wrong side at stitched edge; turn socket side of tape to right side at stitched edge. Press lightly. Edgestitch free edges of snap tape to garment. Join shoulder seams. Trim prefinished collar as in step 1, page 47.

5) Stitch collar to right side of neck edge, with ends at center front. Cut ¾" (2 cm) twill tape 1" (2.5 cm) longer than neck edge. With right sides together and edges even, stitch tape to neck edge over previous stitching. At ends, fold tape to wrong side.

6) Fold twill tape onto garment, encasing the seam allowances. Edgestitch twill tape to garment; backstitch at both ends.

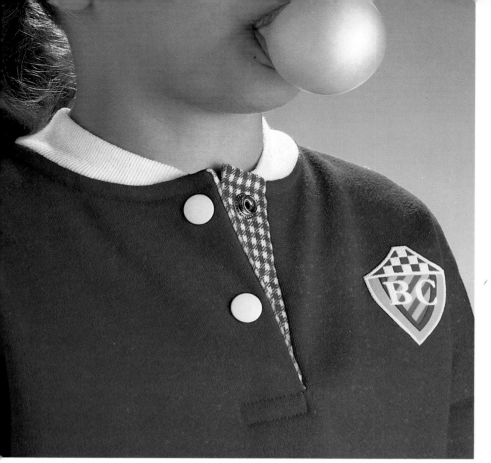

Rugby Plackets

A rugby placket can be added to a basic T-shirt to duplicate a ready-to-wear look. For a girl's garment, mark the placket opening to the left of the center to lap right over left. For a boy's garment, mark the placket opening to the right of center to lap left over right. The center front is at the center of the closed placket. The photos that follow show a girl's shirt.

Face the placket with self-fabric or a coordinating fabric. Interface the placket piece with fusible interfacing. Roll the overlap facing slightly to the outside for a decorative edge.

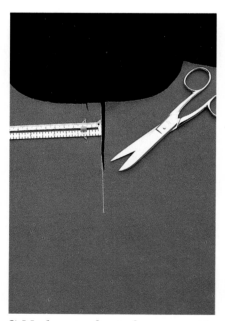

1) Cut placket facing 4½" (11.5 cm) wide by length of opening plus 2" (5 cm); interface. Finish long edges by serging or by stitching with 3-step zigzag. Mark 5" to 6" (12.5 to 15 cm) slash line on right side of facing, 1½" (3.8 cm) from one long edge.

2) Mark center front of garment with clip. Mark 5" to 6" (12.5 to 15 cm) slash line, ⅝" (1.5 cm) to left of center front for girls, right of center front for boys. Cut slash.

3) Pin facing to garment, right sides together, with facing edge ½" (1.3 cm) above neck edge and marked slash line on facing directly under garment opening. Narrow side of facing is on right front for girls, left front for boys.

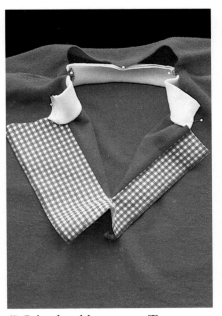

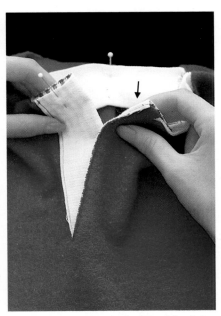

4) Stitch around slash on garment, ⅛" (3 mm) from raw edges, using 12 to 14 stitches per inch (2.5 cm). Shorten stitches near point; make two stitches across point. Cut facing at slash line; clip to stitching at point. Trim facing to match neckline curve.

5) Join shoulder seams. Turn facing to wrong side of garment. Pin collar to neckline, right sides together, so center backs match. Collar ends are ⅝" (1.5 cm) past seam of underlap and at center front mark of overlap.

6) Fold underlap in half, with right sides together. Fold overlap, right sides together, with placket seam about ⅛" (3 mm) from fold (arrow). Stitch neck seam; trim corners.

7) Cut ¾" (2 cm) twill tape for neck edge, so tape is long enough to overlap finished edge of each facing by ½" (1.3 cm). Pin tape over collar with right sides together and edges even; stitch over previous stitching. Turn facings to wrong side; turn tape over neck seam allowances, and pin to garment.

8) Stitch in the ditch (arrow) of underlap seam. Pin the overlap to the garment so about ⅛" (3 mm) of facing is visible at the fold; press. Stitch in the ditch of overlap seam, stitching from lower end to neckline; pivot, and topstitch ¼" (6 mm) from neck seam to secure tape.

9) Close placket; press. Stitch a rectangle ¼" (6 mm) long and the width of placket to secure all layers at lower end of placket. Make bar tack at point of slash by zigzagging in place. Trim excess facing below rectangle of stitching. Apply snaps, or buttons and buttonholes, at center front.

53

Exposed Zippers

You can add color to a shirt by inserting a nonseparating zipper so that the teeth are exposed. Zippers are available in a variety of colors and may be combined with a facing, rolled to the right side to resemble piping. Facings may be made in a contrasting color or a coordinating print, plaid, or striped fabric.

An exposed zipper is inserted in a slash opening in the front of a shirt. Neckline seams finished with twill tape or bias binding are durable, and the tape covers the neckline seam, which will show if the zipper is open.

How to Insert an Exposed Zipper

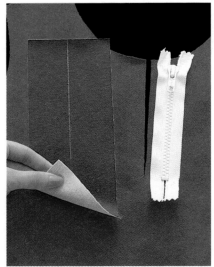

1) Mark center front of garment the length of zipper teeth, plus one seam allowance; slash. Cut facing 3½" (9 cm) wide and 2¼" (6 cm) longer than slash. Interface knit or lightweight facings; mark center line.

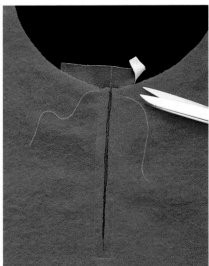

2) Pin facing to garment, right sides together, with ¾" (2 cm) above neck edge and marked line under slash. Stitch ¼" (6 mm) from slash, to ¼" (6 mm) below end of slash; pivot, and stitch ½" (1.3 cm). Pivot; stitch to neck edge. Trim excess facing at neck edge.

3) Cut facing on marked line; clip diagonally to corners. Serge or zigzag raw edges of facing. Turn facing to inside, rolling ⅛" (3 mm) of the facing to right side at slash line; press.

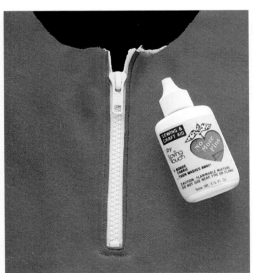

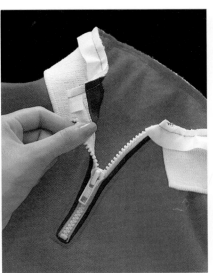

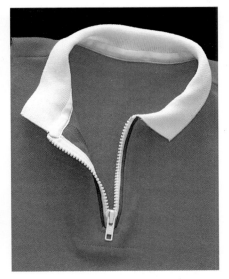

4) Center zipper under opening, with teeth exposed and zipper stop at lower end of opening; glue-baste. Topstitch, using zipper foot, ⅛" to ¼" (3 to 6 mm) from edge, through all layers. Stitch shoulder seams.

5) Apply collar with ends at edge of facing. Cut ¾" (2 cm) twill tape 1" (2.5 cm) longer than neck edge. Pin tape to neck edge, with right sides together and edges even; wrap ½" (1.3 cm) around zipper. Stitch over previous stitching at neck edge.

6) Fold the twill tape onto garment, enclosing the seam allowances. Edgestitch around outer edge of facing and lower edge of tape. Complete garment according to pattern directions.

Pants & Skirts

Pants and skirts are basic items in a child's wardrobe. For ease in sewing as well as comfort in wearing, most children's pants and skirts are sewn with elasticized waistbands, using one of several methods.

For lightweight fabrics, both knits and wovens, a cut-on waistband is most appropriate; most children's patterns are designed this way. The upper edge of the garment is folded down to form a casing for the elastic; the elastic can either be inserted into the casing or sewn directly to the fabric.

Garments made from heavier fabrics, such as fleece or corduroy, may be more comfortable to wear if made with a separate elasticized waistband cut from a lighter-weight fabric, such as ribbing.

Pants and skirts for preschoolers, who no longer need extra fullness to accommodate diapers, are often designed with a smooth-fitting front waistband attached to an elasticized back.

Select elastic carefully; the amount of stretch and the recovery varies with the type of elastic, the method of insertion, and the weight of the fabric (page 16). To determine the minimum length needed for a waistline, stretch the elastic around the widest part of the hips. Determine the maximum length by comfort. As a general rule, elastic will be 2" to 3" (5 to 7.5 cm) shorter than the waist measurement. Heavy fabric hinders elastic recovery; you may want to cut the elastic 1½" (3.8 cm) shorter than usual or apply a lighter-weight separate waistband (page 60).

How to Sew a Cut-on Waistband with Attached Elastic

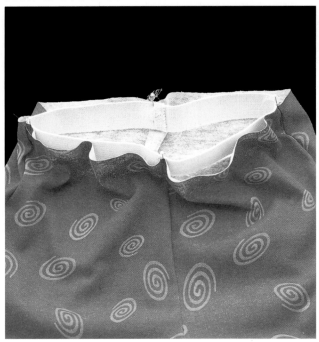

1) **Extend** pattern above waistline two times the elastic width. Cut elastic using guidelines, page 57. Lap elastic ends ½" (1.3 cm); stitch, using zigzag. Pin-mark elastic and garment into fourths. Pin elastic to wrong side of garment, matching pins; align edges.

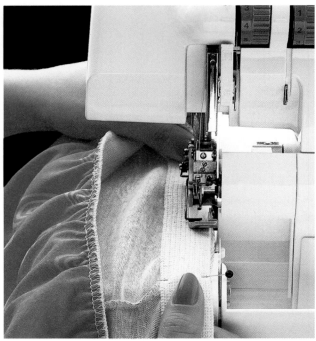

2) **Zigzag** or serge elastic to garment, stretching elastic between pins so garment lies flat; avoid cutting elastic when serging.

3) **Fold** elastic to wrong side of garment so fabric encases elastic. Stitch in the ditch across elastic width at center front, center back, and side seams.

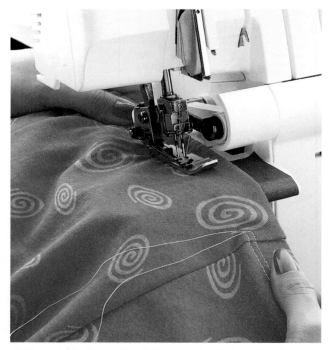

4) **Topstitch** through all layers of waistband at lower edge of elastic, stretching elastic as you sew. Use cover stitch on serger (page 22) or multistitch-zigzag on conventional machine for maximum stretch on knit fabrics. Straight-stitch using long stitches on woven fabrics.

How to Sew a Cut-on Waistband with an Elastic Insert

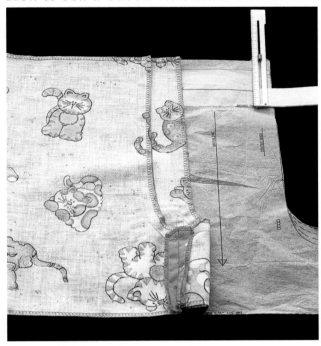

1) **Extend** pattern above waistline twice the elastic width plus ¾" (2 cm). For example, for 1" (2.5 cm) elastic, add 2¾" (7 cm) above the waistline. Cut out garment and stitch together. Finish upper edge, using serger or multistitch-zigzag.

2) **Fold** upper edge to wrong side an amount equal to width of elastic plus ½" (1.3 cm); pin or baste. Edgestitch close to fold.

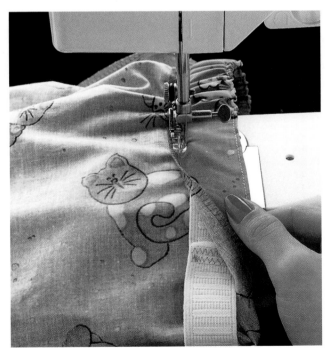

3) **Overlap** ends of elastic ½" (1.3 cm); zigzag. Position elastic within casing area. Stitch next to elastic, using straight stitch and zipper foot; do not catch elastic in stitching. Shift fabric around elastic as necessary while stitching.

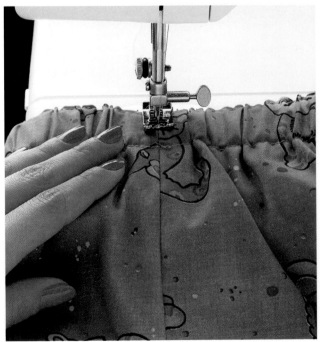

4) **Stretch** waistband to distribute fabric evenly. From right side of garment, stitch in the ditch through all layers at center front, center back, and side seams, to secure elastic.

How to Apply a Separate Elasticized Waistband

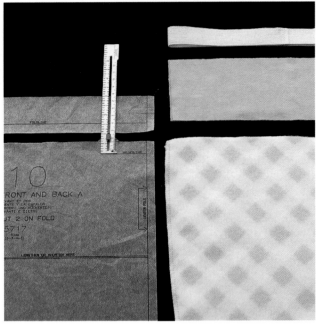

1) Cut garment sections, allowing ⅝" (1.5 cm) seam allowance above waistline. Cut ribbing or lightweight knit, on crosswise grainline, twice the width of the elastic plus 1¼" (3.2 cm); length of waistband must be long enough to pull over hips. Overlap elastic ends; zigzag.

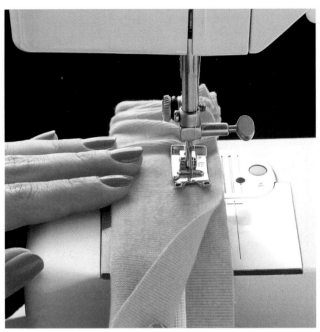

2) Stitch short ends of waistband together. Divide waistband and garment edges into fourths; pin-mark. Fold waistband in half lengthwise, wrong sides together, encasing elastic. Baste ½" (1.3 cm) from raw edges; shift fabric around elastic as necessary.

3) Pin waistband to right side of garment, matching pin marks. Serge just inside basting stitches, stretching waistband to fit garment between pins. Or stitch with conventional machine. Trim seam allowances to ¼" (6 mm); finish seam allowance edges together. Turn seam allowance toward garment.

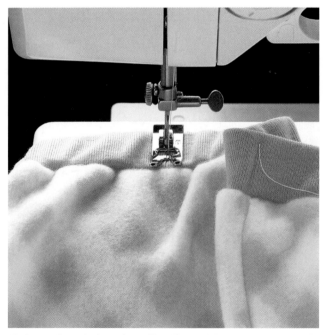

4) Stretch waistband to distribute fabric evenly. Stitch through all layers at center front, center back, and sides to secure elastic.

How to Apply Elastic to a Back Waistband

1) Cut and sew garment front, according to pattern directions. Apply fusible interfacing to front waistband. Stitch to garment front, right sides together; trim seam allowance, and press toward waistband. Trim opposite seam allowance to ¼" (6 mm); finish by serging or using multistitch-zigzag.

2) Extend back pattern above waistline two times the elastic width. Stitch and finish center back seam. Cut elastic 1¼" (3.2 cm) longer than half the amount you would use for fully elasticized waistband. With elastic on wrong side of garment and upper edges even, stitch ends to side seam allowances. Pin center of elastic to center back.

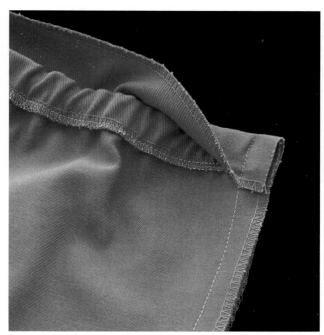

3) Attach elastic; fold to inside and topstitch as in steps 2 and 4, page 58. Complete garment front according to pattern directions. Pin front to back at side seams, right sides together. Turn front waistband over back waistband at side seams; stitch seam.

4) Turn front waistband to inside, encasing elastic ends. Clip back side seam allowance below waistband, if necessary, to press open. Edgestitch around front waistband.

Pockets

Children like pockets, which can be both functional and decorative. Consider the pocket placement and size. Place pockets where the child can easily reach them, and make them large enough to hold objects.

Most styles and shapes of pockets can be used on shirts, jackets, pants, and skirts. Test the shape and size by using a template cut to finished size. Be creative with pocket placement, shape, and trim. Pockets are easier to attach before garment seams are stitched.

Add a kangaroo pocket to shirts and sweatshirts. A kangaroo pocket is a large patch pocket that has side openings. Sew this pocket into the side seams and waistline, and trim the upper edge with piping.

Ribbed-top pockets can be coordinated with knit collars and cuffs. To maintain the original pocket size, shorten the pocket by an amount equal to the finished width of the ribbing.

How to Sew a Kangaroo Pocket

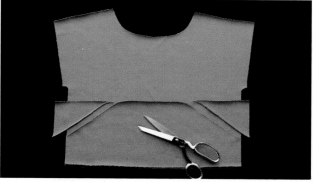

1) Cut pocket the same width as garment and half the garment length from neck edge at center front to lower edge. Cut hand openings at an angle from midpocket on the sides to one-third the width at the upper edge; round the corners at upper edge.

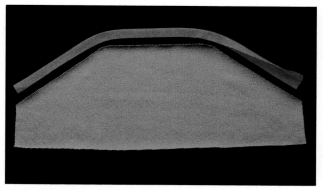

2) Cut fabric strip for piping, 1¼" (3.2 cm) wide and the length of upper edge of pocket; cut on crosswise grain for knits or on bias for wovens. Fold strip in half lengthwise, wrong sides together; press.

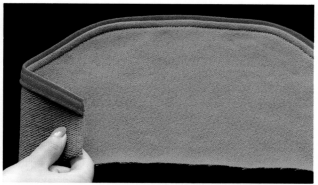

3) Stitch piping to right side of pocket at upper edge, raw edges even, using ⅜" (1 cm) seam. Press seam allowances to wrong side of pocket, with the piping turned up; topstitch the upper edge of pocket ¼" (6 mm) from seam.

4) Glue-baste pocket on garment, matching side seams and lower edge. Topstitch upper edge of pocket, stitching over previous topstitching; do not stitch hand openings closed. Reinforce by stitching in ditch of piping seam; backstitch to strengthen ends.

How to Sew a Ribbed-top Pocket

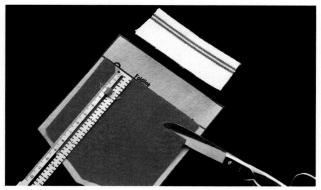

1) Cut pocket with ⅜" (1 cm) seam allowances at sides and lower edge. Trim pocket ¾" (2 cm) below finished upper edge. When using prefinished cuff, cut cuff ½" (1.3 cm) shorter than pocket width and 1¼" (3.2 cm) wide. When using ribbing, cut ribbing ½" (1.3 cm) shorter than pocket width and 2½" (6.5 cm) wide; fold in half lengthwise.

2) Stitch prefinished cuff or ribbing to upper edge of pocket, right sides together, using ¼" (6 mm) seam allowance; stretch cuff or ribbing to fit. Press seam toward pocket; press ⅜" (1 cm) to inside on lower and side edges of pocket. Finish as for basic patch pocket, step 3, page 65.

Patch Pockets

Patch pockets can become a design element of the garment if they are made from a coordinating fabric. You may want to cut pockets from plaid fabric on the bias or from striped fabric on the crosswise grain when the garment is cut on the lengthwise grain. Pockets with straight edges are easier to sew. When adding trim to a pocket, apply it before stitching the pocket to the garment.

Create your own patch pockets of any size or shape, or use the pocket piece provided with the pattern. Check the size and placement of a pocket on the garment by cutting a pocket shape from paper; do not include seam or hem allowances. Mark the pocket placement on the garment with pins or washable marking pen. When creating your own pocket pattern, add seam allowances at the sides and lower edge, and a hem allowance at the upper edge.

A gathered or pleated patch pocket may be made by enlarging a patch pocket pattern. Because of the gathers or pleats, these pockets are more decorative and hold more than standard patch pockets.

How to Make a Basic Patch Pocket

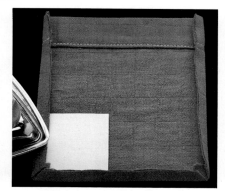

1) Determine finished pocket size; add ⅜" (1 cm) to sides and lower edge, and 1⅜" (3.5 cm) at upper edge. Cut pocket. Press upper raw edge under ⅜" (1 cm), then 1" (2.5 cm); stitch.

2) Place a 2" (5 cm) cardboard template at corner on seamlines. Press ⅜" (1 cm) seam allowances over template; open, and fold diagonally across corner to miter. Refold on pressed lines; press.

3) Glue-baste pocket in place on garment. Edgestitch sides and lower edge. Topstitch ¼" (6 mm) from previous stitching. To bar tack, zigzag at upper corners.

How to Make a Gathered or Pleated Patch Pocket

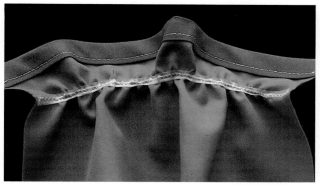

Gathered Pocket. 1) Cut pocket 4" (10 cm) wider than basic patch pocket as in step 2, above. Finish upper edge with double-fold bias tape as in step 1, page 31.

2) Cut ¼" (6 mm) elastic 4" (10 cm) shorter than width of pocket; stitch to pocket 1⅜" (3.5 cm) below upper edge as in steps 1 and 2, page 72.

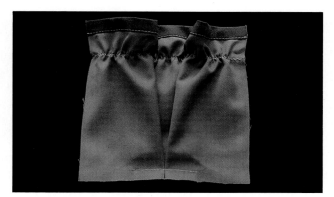

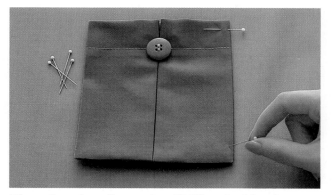

3) Press two 1" (2.5 cm) tucks to center at lower edge of pocket; staystitch. Press seam allowances, and attach pocket as for basic patch pocket, steps 2 and 3, above.

Pleated pocket. Cut pocket 4" (10 cm) wider than basic patch pocket, and finish upper edge as in step 1, above. Press two 1" (2.5 cm) pleats to center of pocket. Center and attach button 1" (2.5 cm) from upper edge, to secure pleats. Press seam allowances, and attach pocket as for basic patch pocket, steps 2 and 3, above.

Faced Patch Pockets

Sew quick and easy faced patch pockets in almost any shape you can imagine; sew animal faces, geometric shapes, flowers, or enlarged motifs from the garment fabric itself. Two tightly spaced rows of stitching make it possible to trim seam allowances close, leaving crisp, smooth edges, even on curves, inner corners, and points.

Use stable woven fabrics for best results. Back light-weight knits with fusible interfacing, and face them with a woven fabric. Plan the pocket design diameter to be at least 4" (10 cm), and determine the location of the pocket opening. For added interest, place the pocket at an angle or embellish it with stitching lines, embroidery, appliqués, or buttons.

How to Make a Faced Patch Pocket

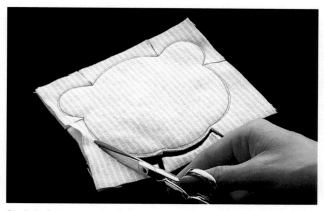

1) Draw pocket design on paper; cut out. Check size and placement on garment. Trace pocket shape on wrong side of pocket fabric; trace mirror image, if pocket is asymmetrical. Draw short perpendicular line at each inner and outer corner. Layer design on lining fabric, right sides together; pin.

2) Stitch on marked line around entire design, using short straight stitches. Stitch second row of stitches just outside first row; at corners, taper stitches into first stitching line. Clip to stitching line at corners; trim fabric away to within 1/8" (3 mm) of stitches.

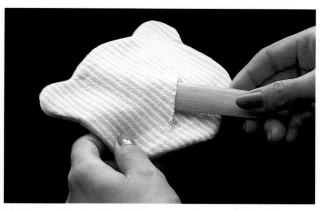

3) Cut small slash in lining, near lower edge. Turn pocket right side out through slash. Use point turner as necessary to smooth outer edges; press.

4) Fuse slash closed, using small strip of fusible interfacing. Embellish pocket as desired. Pin to garment; edgestitch, reinforcing stitches at opening.

Embellishment Techniques

Appliqués. Apply appliqués as on page 94, or use raw-edge method on page 97.

Design lines. Draw design lines on water-soluble stabilizer; pin to pocket front. Stitch over design lines, using short straight stitches or short narrow satin stitches.

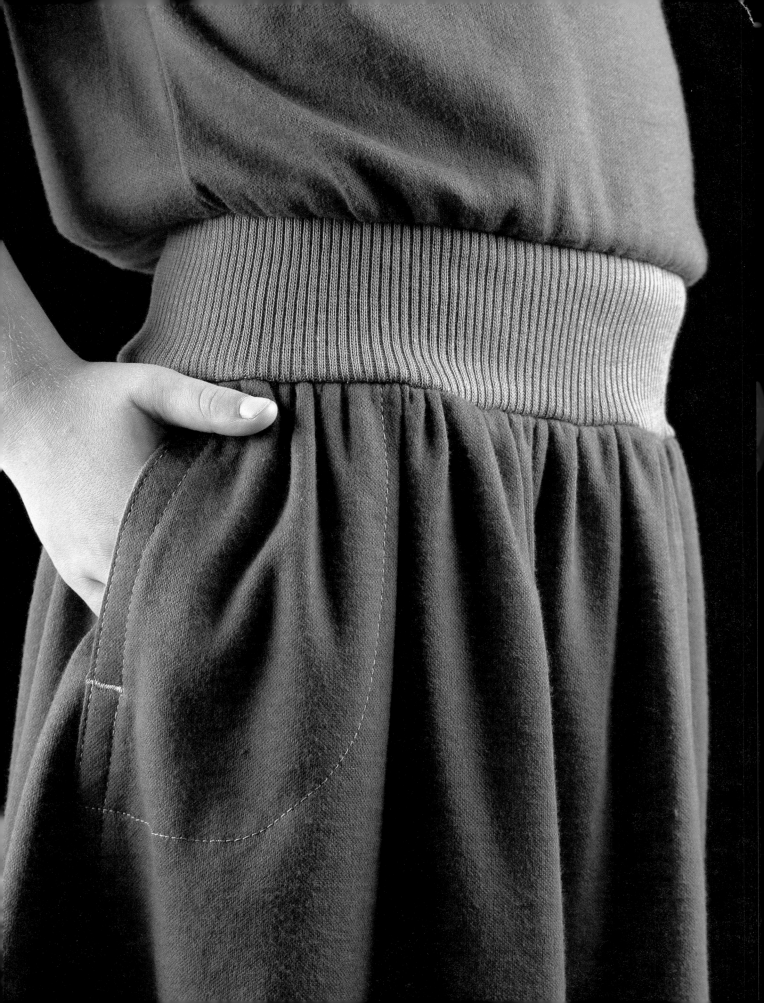

In-seam Pockets

Sew flat, nonbulky in-seam pockets in garment side seams for a ready-to-wear look. Adapt a pattern that has a two-piece pocket by cutting a single pocket piece from self-fabric. In-seam pockets may be either curved or rectangular.

How to Sew One-piece In-seam Pockets

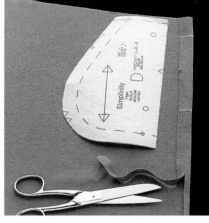

1) Mark pocket opening on side seam allowance of garment front; press to wrong side. Trim seam allowance to ¼" (6 mm).

2) Cut ½" (1.3 cm) twill tape 1" (2.5 cm) longer than pocket opening. Pin tape over trimmed seam allowance at pocket opening, with tape edge next to the fold; stitch through all layers on both edges of twill tape.

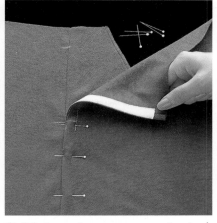

3) Stitch pocket to garment back at side seamline, with right sides together; finish pocket and seam edges. Press seam allowances toward pocket. Lap the garment front over the back side seam allowance, with taped edge even with seamline.

4) Topstitch through all layers above and below pocket opening to match stitching lines on twill tape. Make a bar tack by zigzagging at each end of pocket opening.

5) Pin and straight-stitch the loose edges of pocket to garment front. Repeat steps for other pocket.

6) Complete garment according to pattern directions. Catch upper edge of pocket in waistline seam.

Dresses

Choose construction methods that add a professional finish to the dresses that you sew. Line the yokes of dresses and blouses to eliminate facings that show through the fabric and to add stability to the yoke. Line lightweight or mediumweight fabrics with self-fabric, line bulky fabrics with a lightweight fabric, and line transparent print fabrics with solid-color fabrics. Use narrow French seams on sheer, lightweight fabric. They are used on straight seams, but are unsuitable for curved seams or seams with gathers.

How to Line a Yoke or Bodice

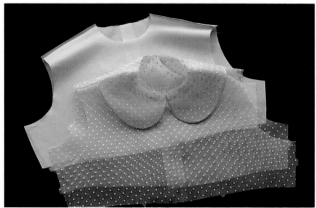

1) Cut yoke and yoke lining. Stitch shoulder seams, using French seams for sheer and lightweight fabrics. Attach collar to right side of yoke.

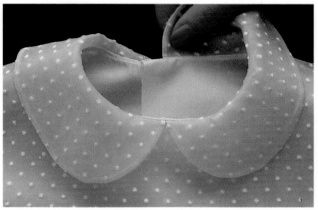

2) Stitch yoke to lining at neckline with right sides together, using short stitch length. Trim the seam allowances to a scant ¼" (6 mm); clip curves, and understitch seam allowances to lining. Turn; press.

3) Pin yoke to lining at lower edge; pin to skirt, right sides together, and stitch. Finish raw edges; press seam allowances toward yoke.

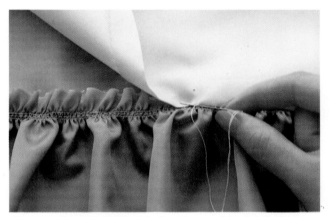

Alternative method. Stitch yoke to skirt, right sides together. Press seam allowances toward yoke. Turn under seam allowance of lining; slipstitch to seam.

How to Sew a Narrow French Seam

1) Mark stitching line in seam allowance, ³⁄₁₆" (4.5 mm) from the seamline. Stitch with *wrong* sides together, using 16 to 18 stitches per inch (2.5 cm).

2) Trim seam allowance to scant ⅛" (3 mm); press seam allowances to one side. Fold on stitching line, *right* sides together; press.

3) Stitch seam ⅛" (3 mm) from fold, encasing raw edges. Press seam allowance to one side.

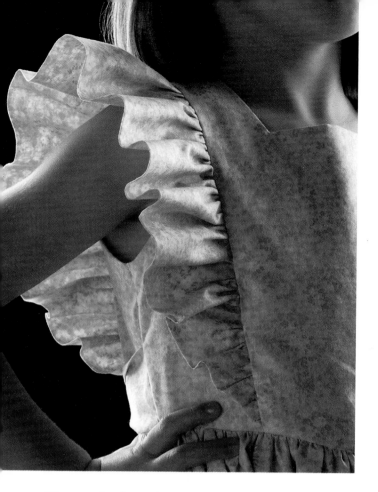

Gathers & Ruffles

Dress patterns often require the techniques of applying elastic, gathering fabric, and making ruffles. The methods that follow can simplify these techniques.

Transparent elastic may be substituted for elasticized casings to gather sleeves and waistlines. Stitch the elastic directly to the garment. The stitches are hidden in the folds of the fabric.

To create soft, fine gathers in lightweight fabrics, stitch gathering lines, using short stitches. To gather a long piece of fabric, you can zigzag stitch over a heavy thread or pearl cotton, which will not break when pulled.

Ruffles may be made from a double or single layer of fabric. Make double-layer ruffles from soft, lightweight fabrics. To cut, fold the fabric, and place the outer edge of the ruffle pattern on the fold to eliminate a hem. The doubled fabric adds body to the ruffle.

Make single-layer ruffles from firm fabrics or fabrics that show through when doubled, such as eyelets and sheer prints. When adding lace to a single-layer ruffle, you may want to reduce the pattern at the outer edge by the width of the lace.

How to Gather Sleeves with Elastic

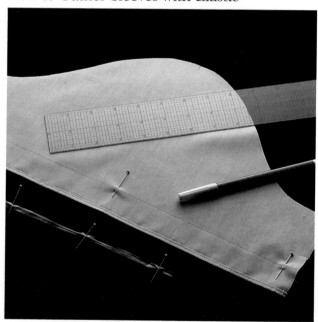

1) Cut ¼" (6 mm) elastic to fit the body comfortably plus seam allowances. Sleeve elastic does not need to fit snugly. Mark stitching line for elastic on wrong side of garment, using washable marking pen. For sleeves, pin-mark elastic and sleeve at seamlines and midpoint; for waistlines, divide elastic and garment into fourths, and pin-mark.

2) Pin elastic to wrong side of garment at pin-marks. Zigzag elastic to garment over marked line; stretch to fit between pins, but do not stretch elastic in seam allowances. Finish garment according to pattern directions, catching elastic in seam.

How to Gather Lightweight Fabrics

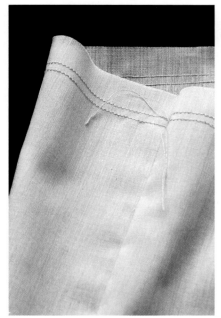

1) Loosen upper tension; set stitch length at 14 to 18 stitches per inch (2.5 cm). Stitch two gathering rows on right side of fabric, 1/8" (3 mm) apart, on each side of seamline.

2) Pull both bobbin threads, and distribute gathers evenly. Stitches automatically pull to wrong side of garment for gathering ease. Wrap threads around a pin to anchor at each end.

3) Stitch on seamline between rows of gathering when joining to garment. Do not remove gathering stitches; outer row of stitches is hidden in fabric fullness.

How to Make Ruffles

Double-layer ruffle. 1) Fold fabric, wrong sides together; place outer seamline or hemline of the ruffle pattern on fold. Cut ruffle. Using a wide zigzag setting, stitch 1/2" (1.3 cm) from raw edges over a heavy thread.

2) Pull heavy thread, and distribute gathers evenly. Wrap thread around a pin to anchor at each end. Stitch ruffle to right side of garment; remove heavy thread.

Single-layer ruffle. Stitch flat lace to outer edge of ruffle, wrong sides together. Trim seam allowance to 1/4" (6 mm); press toward ruffle. Edgestitch 3/8" (1 cm) ribbon over seam allowances through all layers. Gather ruffle.

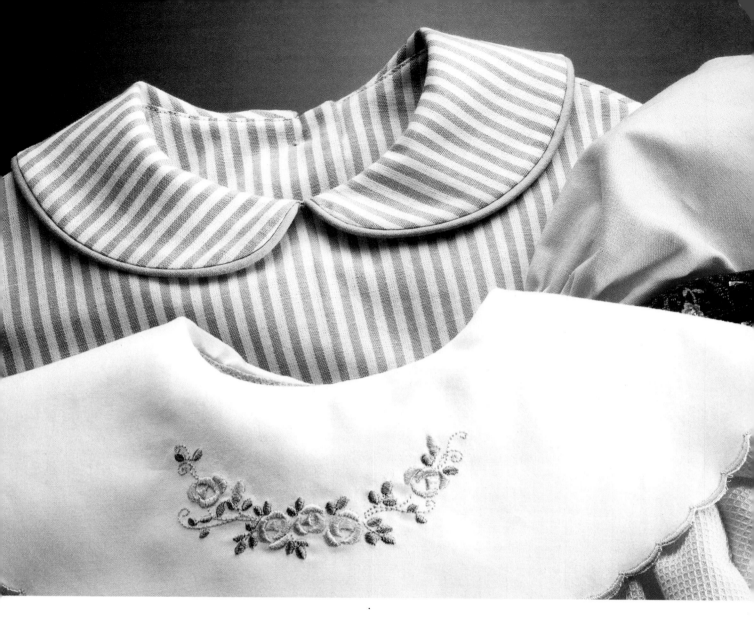

Collars

Add a special detail to the collar to give a dress unique style. Define the outer edge with contrasting piping for a dainty, tailored effect. Add feminine charm with a gathered lace or eyelet edging. Or customize the collar by adding both edge details. Take advantage of the embroidery capabilities of your sewing machine by embellishing a wide collar with a delicate embroidered motif or edging.

Fabrics such as lightweight batiste, broadcloth, calico, organdy, and voile are suitable for collars with decorative edge details. Pipings and trims help stabilize outer collar edges, and may eliminate the need for interfacing on opaque fabrics. To minimize seam or design show-through, back translucent fabrics with sheer knit interfacing.

For a machine-embroidered collar, choose lightweight, tightly woven 100% cotton. Or, if you prefer a sheer look, use silk organza or cotton organdy. Test the embroidery design to help determine the size and placement of the design on the collar; also test the stabilizing method.

Center a large motif on a single layer of fabric for a wide rounded collar. Embroider a continuous scallop design along the outer edge; select one that allows you to easily cut away excess fabric close to the stitches. As an alternate method, stitch a facing to the embroidered collar, and trim the outer edge with piping or gathered lace.

How to Machine-embroider a Single-layer Collar

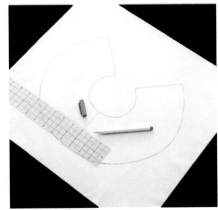

1) Cut fabric larger than pattern, allowing enough excess to fit the piece in embroidery hoop. Trace pattern seamlines onto fabric. Mark center of collar for placement of embroidery.

2) Place fabric in hoop; position under needle. Place tear-away stabilizer under hoop. Embroider center design. Remove from hoop. Stitch decorative border pattern on outer seamline.

3) Tear away stabilizers, taking care not to distort stitches. Apply fray preventer along outer edge of border; allow to dry. Trim close to stitches with small sharp scissors.

Collars with Piping

Piping adds a tailored look to a collar, and may be used for a boy's or girl's collar. String or fine cord is an appropriate filler for piping in children's collars; preshrink the filler. Cut fabric strips for piping, page 103. Collars may also be trimmed with a combination of piping and lace, opposite.

How to Apply Piping to a Collar

1) Cut bias fabric strip 2" (5 cm) wide and length of outer edge of collar. Lay string or fine cord in center, and fold strip in half, wrong sides together. Stitch close to string, using zipper foot. Trim outer edge of collar and bias strip seam allowances to ¼" (6 mm).

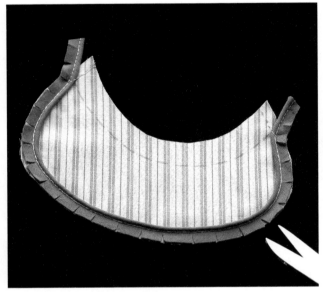

2) Baste piping to right side of upper collar, raw edges even. Clip seam allowance of piping at curves and neckline. Taper piping into seam allowance.

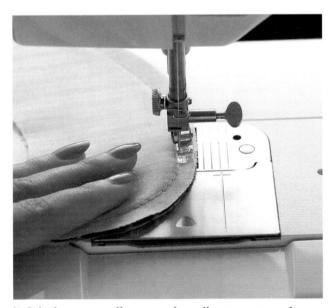

3) Stitch upper collar to undercollar on outer edge, with right sides together; stitch over basting line to join collars and piping.

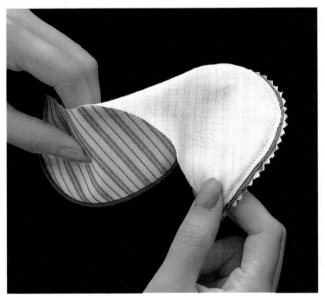

4) Trim undercollar and piping seam allowances to a scant ⅛" (3 mm). Trim upper collar seam allowance slightly with pinking shears; the upper collar seam allowance prevents piping seam allowance from showing through. Turn right side out. Press gently.

Collars with Lace Edging

Lace edging adds a feminine touch to a collar; it may be used alone or with piping (below). To keep the original size of a collar, reduce the width of the pattern by the width of the lace that is to be added at the edge. To make adding trims easier, adjust all seam allowances at the outer edge of the collar to ¼" (6 mm).

How to Apply Lace Edging to a Collar

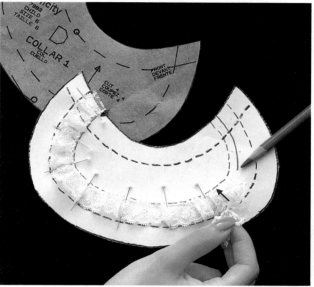

1) **Trace** collar pattern onto paper. Gather straight edge of lace; pin to pattern, with finished edge of lace at pattern seamline. Draw new seamline (arrow) at gathering line of lace. Draw new cutting line ¼" (6 mm) from new seamline. Cut collar, using adjusted pattern.

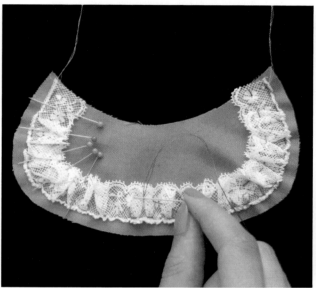

2) **Baste** lace to upper collar, right sides together, placing gathering line at new seamline. Adjust gathers so extra fullness is at curves. Baste ruffled portion of lace down to prevent catching in seam while stitching.

3) **Stitch** upper collar to undercollar on outer edge, right sides together, stitching over basting line to join collars and lace. Trim seam allowances as in step 4, opposite. Turn right side out. Remove basting. Press gently.

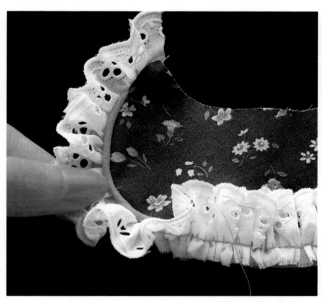

Combining piping and lace. Make adjusted pattern and cut collar as in step 1, above. Baste piping in place, step 2, opposite. Complete collar as in steps 2 and 3, above.

Fleece

Synthetic fleece, such as Polarfleece®, is popular for children's garments. It is warm without being heavy, easy to sew and even easier to launder. It does not ravel, so edge finishes are not necessary, though garment edges are often finished with ribbing (page 48). There are also several decorative edge finishes that give the garment a ready-to-wear look.

When sewing fleece, use a straight stitch length of about 9 stitches per inch (3.5 mm) on the conventional machine. Use ¼" (6 mm) seam allowances whenever possible, and "flatten" the fabric in front of the presser foot, to help feed the bulkiness. Serge fleece, using the widest width and a 3 mm length for flat, durable seams or to flatten an edge before

hemming or binding. Or overlock garment edges using texturized nylon thread for a smooth, flat decorative finish.

When hems are desirable, first serge the hem edge to flatten it; then turn up the hem and stitch ⅛" (3 mm) from the serged edge. Use the serger cover stitch for a professional looking hem. Or, stitch the hem with a twin needle, using the conventional machine. For a decorative effect, stitch the hem from the right side, using an embroidery pattern on the machine.

Take care when pressing fleece. Never allow the iron to rest on the fleece; rather steam the fleece lightly and do the "pressing" with your fingers.

Edge Finishes for Fleece

Scallop-cut edge. Cut fleece, using a rotary cutter with a wave blade. Use this finish on patch pockets or on outer edges of a simple jacket. Create scalloped trim for inserting in a seam, cutting narrow fleece strips with one straight edge and one scalloped edge.

Overlocked edge. Set the serger for a 2-thread overedge stitch with the widest possible width and short stitch length. Use texturized nylon thread in the needle and lower looper. Use the differential feed feature, if available, to stitch evenly around curves, leaving a flat decorative finish.

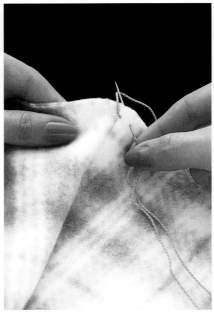

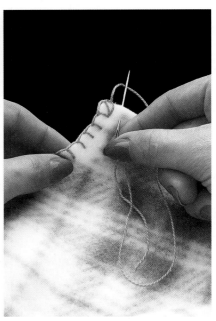

Blanket stitch. 1) Thread single strand #3 pearl cotton, baby yarn, or six strands of embroidery floss onto chenille needle; knot end. Secure to underside at starting point, ¼" (6 mm) from outer edge. Form loop at edge by bringing thread to left and then right as shown; hold loop with left thumb.

2) Insert needle through fabric ¼" (6 mm) from edge, catching garment, if attaching pocket. Bring needle up at edge, passing needle through loop as shown. Pull needle through fabric; release thumb from loop, and pull stitch snug to the fabric edge.

3) Make second stitch ¼" (6 mm) from first stitch, as in steps 1 and 2; continue, working stitches from left to right. Work three stitches at square corners as shown.

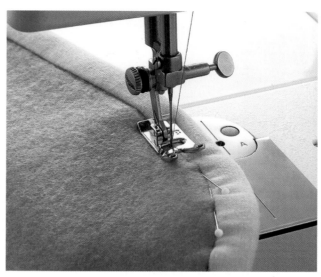

Flat bound edge. 1) Cut binding strips from crosswise grain of lycra/cotton fabric, about four times the desired finished width of the binding. Trim away hem or seam allowance on garment edge. Stitch single layer of binding to fleece, right sides together, at distance from edge equal to desired finished binding width. Ease binding around outside curves; stretch binding slightly on inside curves.

2) Wrap binding to wrong side; pin in the ditch of the seam from the right side, catching binding on the wrong side. Stitch in the ditch of the seam. Trim off excess binding on wrong side close to stitching.

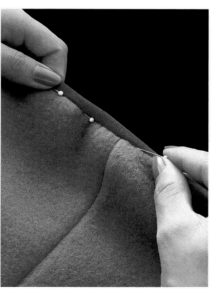

Stretch bound edge. 1) Cut 2½" (6.5 cm) strips of lycra swimwear fabric on lengthwise grain. Fold binding in half lengthwise, right sides together, for shiny side out, or wrong sides together, for dull side. Use flat construction method or in-the-round method, depending on location. Trim away hem or seam allowance on garment edge. Divide binding and garment edge into fourths; pin-mark.

2) Pin binding to right side of garment, matching pins. For best results, serge seam, using widest setting; stretch binding to fit between pins. This flattens seam allowance to minimize bulk. Or sew ¼" (6 mm) straight-stitch seam on conventional machine.

3) Wrap binding to wrong side; pin in the ditch of the seam from the right side, catching binding on the wrong side. Stitch in the ditch of the seam, stretching binding slightly.

Closures

Hook and loop tape. Stitch circles to garment with a triangle, overlapping stitches on one side. Cover stitching on right side with blanket-stitched fleece cutouts, yarn pom-poms, or decorative buttons.

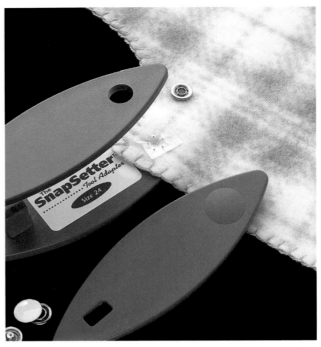

Gripper snaps. Apply snaps, using special tools and following manufacturer's directions. When applying snaps to a single layer of fleece, add support on the underside of the underlap with a small square of interfacing.

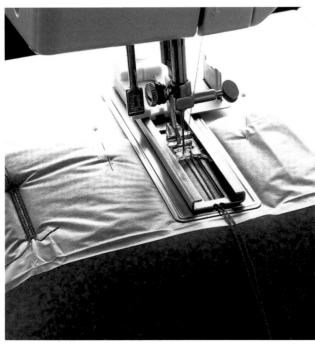

Buttonholes. For best results, sew corded buttonholes in least stretchy direction of fleece. Place water-soluble stabilizer on right side and tear-away stabilizer underneath. Stitch buttonholes; remove stabilizers. Apply liquid fray preventer to stitches before cutting buttonholes open.

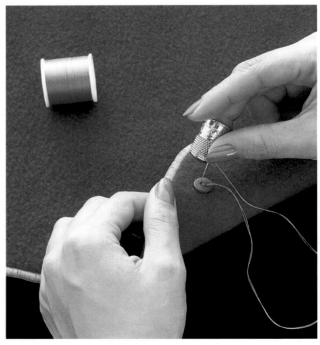

Buttons. When stitching buttons to a single layer of fleece, add support with a small flat button on the underside.

82

Jumpers

Jumpers, jumpsuits, and rompers offer the ease of one-piece dressing and the comfort of clothing that doesn't gap open, come untucked, or hug too tightly around the tummy. For added detail and to eliminate the need for facings, bind armhole and neckline edges in a contrasting color. Use lightweight tightly woven fabric on a woven garment; select single knit, ribbing, or lycra knit to bind edges on knit garments. Or, for easy sewing on stretchy knits, simply turn and stitch the edges, using the cover stitch on the serger

or twin-needle straight stitch with the conventional machine. Both looks are commonly found in ready-to-wear children's clothing.

In garment areas that require an interfaced facing, such as front or back buttoned closures or shoulder straps, stitch the facings to the garment, wrong sides together, before applying the binding. Round any square corners where binding will be applied.

How to Apply Binding

Woven Binding. 1) Stitch any side and shoulder seams. Staystitch neckline and armhole edges ⅛" (3 mm) deeper than seamline. For instance, if garment seam allowances are ⅝" (1.5 cm), staystitch ¾" (2 cm) from edges. Trim away seam allowances.

2) Cut 1" (2.5 cm) bias strips and fold into single-fold bias binding (page 103); press in half. Shape binding to fit curve, using steam iron. Glue-baste binding over raw edges; overlap ends ½" (1.3 cm) on continuous circle.

3) Topstitch over binding, using multistitch-zigzag in thread color to match binding.

Knit Binding. 1) Follow step 1, above. Cut 1" (2.5 cm) binding strips on crosswise grain of knit. Pin binding to garment, right sides together, aligning edges.

2) Overlap binding ends on continuous circle. Turn under ½" (1.3 cm) at finished garment edge. Serge or stitch binding to garment ¼" (6 mm) from edge.

3) Wrap binding to underside; glue-baste. Stitch in the ditch from right side, catching binding on underside. Trim binding close to stitching.

How to Finish Edges with the Turn and Stitch Method

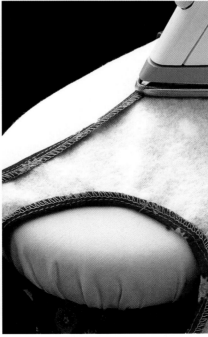

1) Stitch any side and shoulder seams. Staystitch neckline and armhole edges in seam allowance, just inside seamline.

2) Trim the seam allowances to ⅜" (1 cm). Turn any facings to right side, and stitch seam. Turn to inside, and press. Press seam allowances to underside.

3) Topstitch neckline and armhole edges, using twin needle stitch on conventional machine or cover stitch on serger.

Reversible Vest with Bow Tie

Coordinate a reversible vest with a bow tie. For the vest, select two fabrics that are similar in weight and have the same care requirements. Interface the entire vest front for a crisp look and for support in the closure area. Gripper snaps, attached with a decorative prong for both the ball and socket, allow the vest to lap correctly when reversed.

For an easy-to-sew bow tie, cut fabric either on the bias or straight grain. Cut fabric for the bow 3½" × 9" (9 × 23 cm), for the knot 3" × 2" (7.5 × 5 cm), and for the neck band 2½" (6.5 cm) wide by the length of the neck measurement plus 1½" (3.8 cm). (Take neck measurement over the shirt.) For interfacing, cut a piece of polyester fleece, 1½" × 9" (3.8 × 23 cm). Attach hook and loop tape to the ends of the neck band for easier dressing. This size will be appropriate up to a Boys' size 10.

How to Make a Bow Tie

1) Fold all fabric strips lengthwise, with right sides together, and stitch with ¼" (6 mm) seam; press open. Turn the strips right side out; press flat, centering seam.

2) Insert fleece in strip for bow. Fold ends of strip to center back, overlapping ends ¼" (6 mm); stitch. Wrap center of bow tightly with double thread. Tack center back of bow to center of neck band.

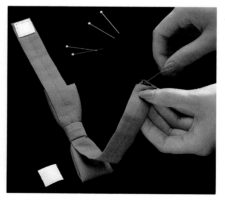

3) Wrap strip for knot around bow and neck band, lapping ends; hand-stitch in place. On ends of neck band, turn in raw edges ¼" (6 mm). Stitch hook and loop tape to ends of neck band.

How to Make a Reversible Vest

1) Cut two fronts and one back from fabric; repeat, using coordinating fabric. Follow pattern directions to attach pockets to interfaced vest front. Stitch all shoulder seams; press open.

2) Stitch vests together at front, neck, and armhole edges, right sides together, matching shoulder seams. Trim seam allowances to ¼" (6 mm); clip curves to stitching. Press seams open.

3) Turn vest right side out by pulling front through shoulder to back, one side at a time. Press, positioning seamline exactly on the edge.

4) Stitch side seams of both layers in one continuous step, matching armhole seams. Press seams open. Trim seam allowances to ⅜" (1 cm).

5) Stitch lower raw edges, with right sides together and side seams matching; leave 3" (7.5 cm) opening for turning. Trim seam allowances to ¼" (6 mm); trim corners.

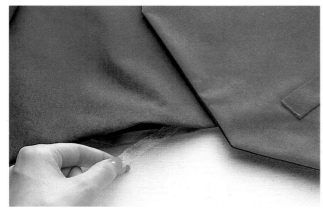

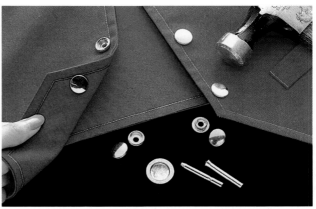

6) Turn vest right side out through opening at lower edge. Press lower edge, positioning seamline exactly on the edge. At opening, turn in raw edges, and fuse. Topstitch vest ¼" (6 mm) from edges, if desired.

7) Mark snap positions on both sides of each vest front. Apply snaps according to package directions, using decorative caps on both parts of snaps.

Separating Zippers

Use exposed separating zippers as a decorative touch in children's sweatshirts or jackets made from warm, durable fabrics, such as corduroy, denim, sweatshirt fleece, and double-faced polyester bunting.

Before applying a zipper, complete the garment, including the collar and lower edge, according to pattern directions. Trim front opening seam allowances to ⅜"(1 cm), and trim the neck seam allowance to ¼" (6 mm). Finish neckline and zipper tapes with bias binding for a neat, decorative trim.

If the correct zipper size is not available, purchase a zipper longer than needed. The zipper can be trimmed to fit during application.

How to Apply a Separating Zipper

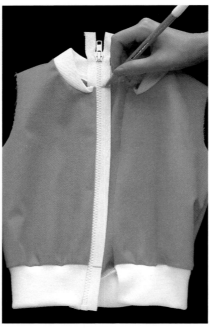

1) Trim neck and front opening seam allowances, above. Pin one side of open zipper to jacket edge, right sides together and edges even, with bottom stop at lower edge. Stitch next to zipper teeth from lower edge to neckline; leave excess zipper at neck edge.

2) Close zipper, and mark the alignment of seams or the fabric design. Open zipper. Matching marks on zipper to jacket, pin and stitch other side of zipper as in step 1.

3) Cut two bias strips (page 103), 2⅛" (5.3 cm) wide and 1" (2.5 cm) longer than zipper opening. Cut another bias strip, 1⅝" (4 cm) wide and length of neck edge. Press all strips in half lengthwise, wrong sides together.

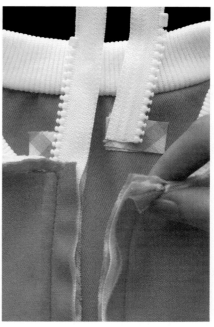

4) Place binding over zipper tape, with raw edges of binding and zipper even. Wrap ½" (1.3 cm) of binding tightly around zipper at lower end; leave ½" (1.3 cm) excess binding at neck edge. Stitch from lower edge over previous stitching.

5) Pivot, and stitch along the neck seamline to fold of binding. If zipper is longer than opening, turn handwheel by hand to stitch between zipper teeth.

6) Trim excess binding even with raw edge of neckline. Trim excess zipper one tooth beyond stitching line. Repeat binding application for other side.

7) Place binding over collar, with raw edges even. Extend the ends of the neckline binding ¼" (6 mm) onto the zipper binding; trim excess. Stitch the neckline binding over previous stitching.

8) Fold bindings to the wrong side. Baste bindings to garment on fold. Edgestitch folded edge of binding to jacket front, beginning at the lower edge. Pivot at fold of the neckline binding.

9) Continue stitching around the fold of neckline binding and down other front binding fold. Bar tack at bottom of zipper by zigzagging in place.

Personalizing

Adding a Personal Touch

Use your imagination to create personal touches that will make a garment special to the child. The techniques for personalizing clothing can be adapted to a single garment or repeated on several garments in a coordinated wardrobe.

Consider color blocking, especially when you are sewing more than one garment; use the remnants from one garment for blocks of color in another. Or highlight and coordinate garments with piping. You may want to add appliqués; select either the traditional method of appliqué on page 94, or the quick and easy raw-edge method on page 97.

Patchwork trims can add greatly to the cost of ready-to-wear garments, but some techniques permit you to make designs with small amounts of fabric in a short time. Fabric paints may be used to personalize a garment. They can also be used to decorate fabric shoes.

When personalizing children's garments, remember that special touches can be added to fronts, backs, and sides of garments, and all trims must be attached securely and safely.

Tips for Placement of Design

Balance design shapes. For example, you can offset a small design at the upper left of a shirt with a larger design at the lower right.

Place a placket at a shoulder or raglan seam so a design can be centered on a shirt front.

Add a design to the back of a shirt that has a plain front, or repeat a design used on the front.

Machine-stitch trim to sleeves while the piece is still flat to eliminate the need for handwork in areas too small for your sewing machine to reach.

Decorate sleeves using elbow patches or by placing designs down the center of the sleeve.

Highlight shoulder seams with piping, twill or bias tape, or ribbing.

Repeat a design to make a border at the neckline, yoke, or hemline.

Create interest with fabric strips or trims placed diagonally, vertically, or horizontally; an uneven number of strips or trims may be more pleasing than an even number.

Appliqués

Appliqués are a traditional method for decorating children's garments. Select from three basic types of appliqués; purchase iron-on or sew-on appliqués, or design your own. For a fast and easy decorative touch, fuse purchased iron-on appliqués to a garment, following the manufacturer's directions. Purchased sew-on appliqués may be fused to the garment using fusible web. You may wish to topstitch to secure the appliqué through many launderings.

You may want to design your own custom-made appliqués. Look at magazines, ready-to-wear garments, or coloring books for ideas. Fruit, animals, numbers, toys, hearts, and rainbows are all popular shapes for children's appliqués. Consider cutting motifs from printed fabrics.

Before assembling the appliqué, plan the work sequence. Smaller pieces may need to be positioned on and stitched to larger pieces before applying appliqué to the garment, and some pieces may overlap other pieces.

Embellish the appliqués with bows, buttons, ribbons, pom-poms, fabric paint, or cord. Cut ends of cord may be placed under appliqué pieces before fusing. Trims may be stitched or glued in place, using permanent fabric glue.

Tips for Appliqués

Practice stitching an appliqué on a test piece before working with the garment piece.

Select a colorfast fabric for an appliqué that is compatible with garment fabric in weight and care requirements; preshrink all fabrics.

Remember that it is easiest to stitch around large, simple shapes with few corners.

Leave a fabric margin in a geometric shape around intricate motifs cut from printed fabrics.

Apply paper-backed fusible web to the wrong side of the appliqué fabric before cutting out the shape.

Add durability to a garment by applying an appliqué with fusible web at knees or elbows.

Add ½" (1.3 cm) to sides of appliqué pieces that will go under another piece; trim to reduce bulk when final placement is determined.

Remember that shapes drawn on paper backing of fusible web will be reversed on the garment; draw mirror images of letters or numbers.

Apply tear-away stabilizer to the wrong side of a garment for smooth satin stitching at the edge of an appliqué.

Use a special-purpose presser foot with a wide channel to prevent buildup of satin stitches

Apply an appliqué to garment before joining seams. It is easier to apply an appliqué while fabric is flat.

How to Make and Apply an Appliqué

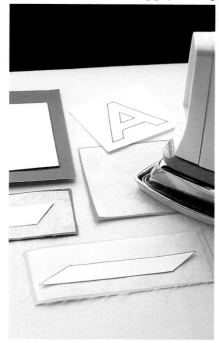

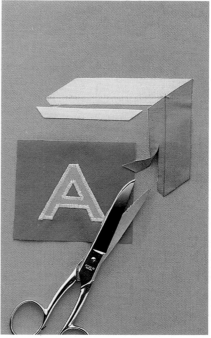

1) Apply paper-backed fusible web to wrong side of appliqué fabric, following manufacturer's directions. Allow fabric to cool.

2) Draw design on fabric or paper backing; add ½" (1.3 cm) to sides of appliqué pieces that go under another piece. Cut out design and remove paper backing.

3) Position appliqué pieces on the garment fabric. Trim appliqué pieces under other pieces to reduce bulk; leave scant ¼" (6 mm). Fuse appliqué pieces to garment.

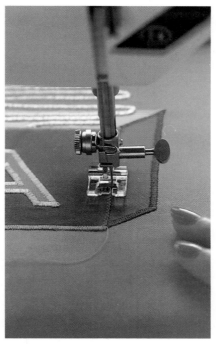

4) Cut tear-away stabilizer 1" (2.5 cm) larger than appliqué. Glue-baste to the wrong side of garment, under appliqué. Zigzag stitch around appliqué, using short, narrow stitches.

5) Decrease the upper tension, and adjust stitches for short, wide zigzag; satin stitch around appliqué edges to cover all raw edges. Remove tear-away stabilizer.

Appliqué with squeaker. Apply fusible interfacing to wrong side of appliqué. Place squeaker under appliqué; glue appliqué in place at edges. Complete appliqué as in steps 4 and 5, left.

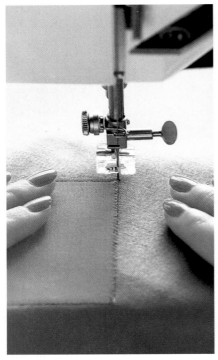

Outside corners. Stitch past the edge of the appliqué one stitch. Raise presser foot, pivot fabric, and continue stitching.

Inside corners. Stitch past corner a distance equal to width of satin stitch. Raise presser foot, pivot fabric, and continue stitching.

Curves. Pivot fabric frequently. For outside curves, pivot with needle on outer edge of stitching (**a**); for inside curves, pivot with needle at inner edge of stitching (**b**).

Appliqués from printed fabric. Cut designs from fabric to use as appliqués. For an intricate design, cut a fabric margin in a simple shape.

Decorated appliqués. Decorate an appliqué with buttons, bows, beads, ribbons, or pom-poms. Stitch the decorations securely.

Padded appliqués. Sew small padded appliqués as for wall sculptures, page 119. Stitch them to garment along interior design lines, for a dimensional look.

Raw-edge Appliqués

Raw-edge appliqués are quick and easy. For ease in sewing, stitch the appliqués in place before constructing the garment. Stitch intricate shapes to the garment fabric, using free-motion machine stitching techniques. Drop or cover the feed dogs on the machine, and guide the fabric by hand in order to stitch in any direction without repositioning the fabric.

How to Sew a Raw-edge Appliqué

1) Stiffen the fabric, using spray starch. Cut out desired shapes. Arrange shapes over fabric; secure in place with glue stick.

2) Place tear-away stabilizer under fabric. Stitch ⅛" (3 mm) from raw edges, using a darning foot and free-motion stitching; use your hands to guide the fabric as you stitch. Stitch any interior design lines.

Alternative method. Follow step 1, left. Stitch around simple shapes, using short, wide multistitch-zigzag.

Fabric Painting & Printing

Fabric paints, inks, and fabric crayons can be used to decorate garments. Some methods, including stenciling, stamping, and crayon heat transfer are easy enough for children to do under supervision. Help children plan and practice their own designs before they begin painting on fabric. Wash and dry the fabric to remove any sizing before applying the design. Decorate the fabric before cutting out the pattern, or decorate the completed garment.

Select acrylic fabric paints for projects painted by children. The cleanup of these water-soluble paints is easy while the paint is wet. Paint jumbo stencils on fabric, using cellulose sponges or foam pouncers. Stamp images onto fabric using large rubber stamps, such as Chunky Stamps® from Back Street. Or use precut sponge shapes. Look for heat transfer designs that supply only the outline of the image, and color them in with fabric paint pens, such as Dylon ColorFun®, by Dritz. Have a child create original artwork, using heat transfer crayons on paper, and transfer the design to a new shirt.

Follow the manufacturers' directions for each product. Drying times will vary, and some products should be heat set to make them permanent. Lay garments or fabric flat when painting, and place wax paper or smooth cardboard between layers to prevent color from bleeding through.

How to Stencil on Fabric

1) Place the garment flat on clean paper, with wax paper between fabric layers. Use purchased stencil design or cut an original design from thin cardboard. Tape stencil in position on garment.

2) Dilute stencil paint, using one drop of water to ten drops of paint. Dampen sponge; squeeze until almost dry. Dip sponge in paint, and use to paint inside stencil. Lift stencil gently. Heat-set according to manufacturer's directions.

Alternative method. Cut sponge into desired shape. Dampen the sponge; squeeze until almost dry. Dip sponge in paint, and apply to garment. Allow garment to dry flat. Heat-set according to the manufacturer's directions.

Techniques with Fabric Paint

Spread thin layer of paint on paper plate; press jumbo rubber stamp into paint. Press onto fabric, printing paint; lift straight up from fabric. Apply more paint to stamp with each print.

Color desired design on paper, using heat-transfer crayons. Avoid letters or numbers, as image will be reversed when applied to fabric. Place paper face-down on fabric; transfer design, using iron and following manufacturer's directions.

Transfer design outline onto fabric, using light box, heat-transfer marking pen, or purchased heat-transfer design. Color design using fabric pens.

Use a child's hand for printing on fabric. In shallow pan, mix paint solution of one drop water and ten drops paint. Dip hand in paint; place on fabric. Press down on fingers and palm; lift hand straight up. Heat-set paint if recommended by manufacturer.

Color & Design Blocking

Create a distinctive look with color and design blocking. Choose two or more fabrics to use in one garment; plan the fabric arrangement, and cut individual pattern pieces from each fabric. Or trace a pattern piece, cut the traced pattern apart, and cut each piece from a different fabric. Choose a simple pattern design. For variety, you can mix woven and knit fabrics, or solids and prints. Combine colorfast fabrics that are compatible in weight and have similar care requirements.

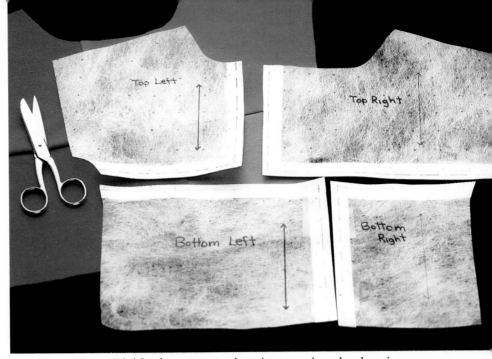

Adapt a pattern. Divide the pattern piece into sections by drawing new seamlines; cut pattern apart, and add ¼" (6 mm) seam allowance at new seams. Join sections before completing the garment.

Combine woven and knit fabrics. When using a pattern designed for knit fabric, use woven fabric in areas that will not affect wearing ease, such as collars, cuffs, yokes, and pockets.

Combine striped fabrics. Cut pattern pieces from two or more striped fabrics, each with stripes of a different size. Combine stripes horizontally, vertically, or diagonally.

Piping

Piping adds a decorative touch at garment seams or edges. Use it on pockets, collars, side seams of pants and skirts, shirt yoke seams, and seams of raglan sleeves. Combine piping with color blocking (page 101) and topstitching for interesting effects.

Make piping from either woven or knit fabric. Cut woven fabric on the bias; cut knit fabric on the crosswise or lengthwise grain. Use fabric that is colorfast and requires care similar to that of the garment. Preshrink fabric and the cord or yarn used as the filler in the piping.

Before cutting the fabric strips for piping, decide whether the piping will be filled or flat. For a soft, yarn-filled piping or a firmer, cord-filled piping, the fabric width should be at least two seam allowances plus the circumference of the filler, plus ⅛" (3 mm). For a flat ⅛" (3 mm) piping, cut the width of the fabric strip at least two seam allowances plus ¼" (6 mm). The finished piping seam allowances should be the same width as those of the garment. When using ¼" (6 mm) seam allowances on the garment, it is easier to sew the piping with ⅝" (1.5 cm) seam allowances, and trim them later to match the garment.

How to Sew Piping

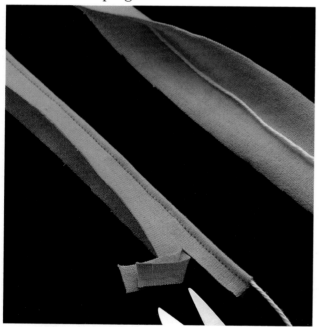

Filled piping. 1) Center cord or yarn on wrong side of fabric strip. Fold strip in half lengthwise, wrong sides together, enclosing cord. Stitch close to cord, using zipper foot; stretch woven fabric slightly as you sew. Trim seam allowances to match those of garment.

2) Pin piping to right side of garment, with raw edges even. Curve ends of piping into seam allowance at inconspicuous place, so ends overlap and piping tapers to raw edge. For enclosed seams, such as collar seams, taper piping into seam allowance at intersection of seams, step 2, page 76.

How to Prepare Bias Strips

1) Fold fabric diagonally, so straight edge on crosswise grain is parallel to selvage. Cut on fold for first bias edge. Use ruler and rotary cutter to cut 2" (5 cm) strips.

2) Piece strips, if necessary. Pin strips in V shape, with right sides together and short ends aligned. Stitch ¼" (6 mm) seam; press seam open. Trim seam allowances even with bias strip.

Single-fold bias tape. Prepare bias strip, left. Trim one end to a point. Pull bias strip through bias tape maker; press folds to center as strip comes out end of tape maker.

3) Stitch on seamline. Remove stitching in piping at ends; trim cord in seam allowance. Stitch garment seam over previous stitching line, with piping between right sides of garment pieces.

Flat piping. Use 1" (2.5 cm) single-fold bias tape for ⅛" (3 mm) finished piping and ⅝" (1.5 cm) seam allowances. Press tape open; fold in half lengthwise, and press. Pin piping to garment, and stitch seam as in steps 2 and 3, left.

Patchwork Trims

Versatile patchwork trims can be made from small amounts of woven fabrics. Use coordinating colors and the garment fabric, if desired, for diagonal or Seminole patchwork trims. Stitch the fabric strips together on the straight grain for either type of trim. Diagonal patchwork trims can be constructed faster, and from less fabric, than Seminole patchwork trims.

Constructing Seminole patchwork trims is not difficult, but this method of piecing does require precise measuring, cutting, and stitching. A rotary cutter and ruler help you to cut strips accurately.

To vary the size of Seminole patchwork trims, vary the size of the squares. For a border, sew wide strips at the edges, or cut a border strip on the straight grain, and sew it to the Seminole patchwork trim.

Diagonal or Seminole patchwork trims may be applied to garments in several ways. Insert them as stripes or garment borders, or use color blocking techniques (page 101). An entire yoke, bib, or other pattern piece may be cut from a patchwork trim.

How to Make a Diagonal Patchwork Trim

1) Cut fabric strips on straight grain the finished width plus two ¼" (6 mm) seam allowances. Cut two strips each of three or more fabrics; widths of strips may vary. Stitch strips together lengthwise, with right sides together and in desired sequence, repeating the pattern once.

2) Press seams in one direction. Cut pieced fabric into bias strips, and stitch strips together as necessary, step 2, page 103. Attach to garment, being careful not to stretch strip.

How to Make a Seminole Patchwork Trim

1) Measure, and cut fabric strips on straight grain the finished width plus two ¼" (6 mm) seam allowances. Join strips in sequence, right sides together; stitch accurate seams. Press seams in one direction.

2) Cut pieced fabric into strips. The width of each strip should be equal to the width of center strip as cut in step 1, left.

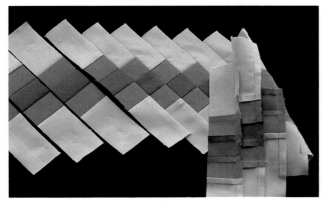

3) Join strips, right sides together; use ¼" (6 mm) seams and stagger color blocks to form diagonal pattern. Alternate direction of seam allowances on strips to help match seams. Edges along sides are staggered. Press seams in one direction.

4) Trim long sides even. To add a border, cut two edging bands of straight-grain self-fabric or coordinating fabric; stitch to long sides of patchwork trim, right sides together.

Decorating the Nursery

When you plan the decor of a nursery, you may want to consider using neutral colors for wallpaper and paint. Save colorful decorating touches for the accessories, which can easily be changed or adapted as the child grows. Pastel colors are the traditional choice for a nursery, but do not overlook other choices, such as bold primary colors.

You can find many decorating ideas for nurseries in magazines, decorating books, and wallpaper and fabric stores. Select a theme to unify the nursery, and use your creative skills and sewing ability for projects such as appliqué, trapunto, or stenciling.

Adorable crib ensembles that include a skirt, fitted sheet, bumper pad, and coverlet are both afford-able and unique when you sew them yourself. Look for coordinat-ing fabrics that have all the features a new baby could want; cheerful colors, soft, cozy surface texture, and washability. Decorator fabrics, though generally labeled "dry clean only", offer a wide range of design options. Many 100% cottons may be washed successfully, though. Test-wash a sample of the decorator fabric for color retention and to determine the amount of shrink-age, and purchase additional length as necessary. Preshrink all fabrics and findings before you begin construction.

Crib Skirt

Crib skirts, designed to hide the metal springs under the mattress, can be sewn to match or coordinate with the bumper pad and coverlet. Unlike the three-sided versions for beds, a crib skirt covers the sides, foot, and head of the crib and splits at each corner to fit over the spring supports. The directions are for a skirt that drops 14" (35.5 cm) below the mattress, though you can make it longer or shorter, if you prefer.

To limit the number of seams in the skirt, select fabric that can be railroaded. This means that the lengthwise grain of the fabric runs horizontally around the skirt. The design is then turned sideways, so railroading is only suitable for solid colors or nondirectional prints.

✂ Cutting Directions

Cut the fabric length into three long strips, cutting on the lengthwise grain. The cut width of each strip is 15" (38 cm) for a finished crib skirt of 14" (35.5 cm). Cut 18" (46 cm) from the ends of two of the strips, for the skirt side sections. Cut the remaining strip in half, for the head and foot sections. Cut the muslin to the same size as the mattress support plus 1" (2.5 cm) in each direction, for the deck.

YOU WILL NEED

> **3½ yd. (3.2 m) fabric that can be railroaded,** at least 45" (115 cm) wide, for skirt.
>
> **1⅝ yd. (1.5 m) muslin,** for deck.

How to Sew a Crib Skirt

1) Turn under and stitch ½" (1.3 cm) double-fold hem along lower edge of each skirt section. Then turn under and stitch ½" (1.3 cm) double-fold hem on both ends of each section.

2) Zigzag over a cord on the right side at upper edge of each section, within seam allowance. For more control when adjusting gathers, zigzag over a second cord ¼" (6 mm) from first row. Mark center of each side section; repeat for sides of deck.

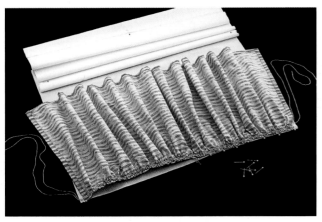

3) Align upper edge of one side section to edge of deck, right sides together, matching center marks; place hemmed ends ½" (1.3 cm) from corners. Pull on gathering cords, and gather section evenly to fit. Pin in place. Repeat for remaining three sides.

4) Stitch ½" (1.3 cm) from raw edges. Serge ½" (6 mm) closer to edges, trimming excess. Or stitch again ¼" (6 mm) closer to edges; trim close to stitching, and finish raw edges by zigzagging. Press seam toward deck.

Bumper Pad

To protect baby's precious head and keep legs and arms from slipping between the side rungs of the crib, sew a bumper pad. These bumper pads are designed to fit a crib with an inside measurement of 54" × 31" (137 × 78.5 cm). Extra fabric is allowed in the corners to make it adjustable for slightly larger or smaller cribs. For easy washing, a continuous zipper is inserted in the bottom of the bumper pad to allow the foam inserts to be removed. If necessary, the inserts can be washed separately. Simply toss them in the washing machine and allow them to air-dry.

✂ Cutting Directions

Cut six pieces of foam, 25" × 8" (63.5 × 20.5 cm). Cut six foam covers from muslin, 28" × 21½" (71 × 54.8 cm). Cut four 53" × 10" (134.5 × 25.5 cm) pieces of fabric for the sides. Cut four 30" × 10" (76 × 25.5 cm) pieces of fabric for the ends. For the boxing strip, cut 2¾" (7 cm) fabric strips on the crosswise grain; piece the strips together as necessary to make one 179" (454.7 cm) strip. For welting, cut 2" (5 cm) bias strips, and piece them together to make 4¾ yd. (4.35 m). For the ties, cut 2" (5 cm) bias strips, and piece them together to make ¾ yd. (0.7 m).

YOU WILL NEED

Polyurethane foam, 2" (5 cm) thick.

2½ yd. (2.3 m) muslin, for foam insert covers.

2½ yd. (2.3 m) fabric, for sides.

1¼ yd. (1.15 m) fabric, for boxing strip and ties.

1 yd. (0.95m) fabric; 4¾ yd. (4.35 m) cording, for welting, or 4¾ yd. (4.35 m) purchased welting.

Continuous zipper, 162" (411.5 cm) long, with two zipper pulls.

How to Cover Foam Inserts

1) Fold insert cover in half lengthwise. Stitch ½" (1.3 cm) seam along long side and one short end. Trim corners. Turn right side out. Repeat for remaining covers.

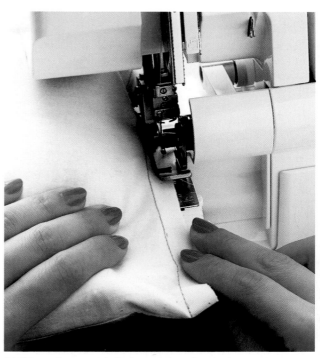

2) Wrap foam with lightweight plastic; insert into lining, and pull plastic away. Stitch remaining short end closed; finish raw edges together, using serger or zigzag stitch.

How to Sew a Bumper Pad

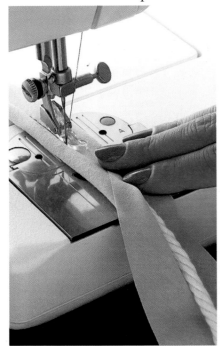

1) Center cording on wrong side of bias strip. Fold strip over cord, aligning raw edges. Using zipper foot on right side of the needle, machine baste close to cord, gently stretching bias.

2) Fold edges of bias strip for ties to center, using bias-fold tape maker (page 103); press. Fold strip in half again; press. Edgestitch next to folds.

3) Cut strip into five sections 24" (61 cm) long and two sections 12" (30.5 cm) long. Knot both ends of long ties and one end of short ties.

4) Stitch head and side pieces together into two strips for the inside and outside of the bumper pad, using ½" (1.3 cm) seam allowances. Strips are mirror images of each other. Mark centers of long sections.

5) Cut 162" (411.5 cm) of continuous zipper coil. Mark bar tack placement 1½" (3.8 cm) from one end of zipper. Open zipper about 1" (2.5 cm). Cut a notch to within ½" (1.3 cm) of mark.

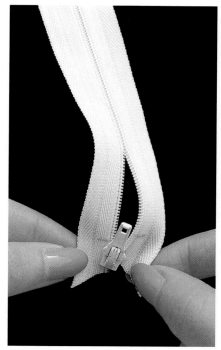

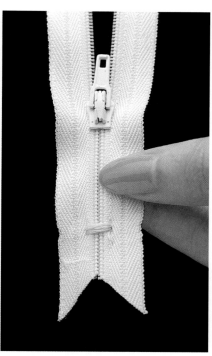

6) Insert one side of zipper coil into shaped end of zipper pull, with flat side of coil and tab of zipper pull facing up; insert other side, gently working coil into zipper pull.

7) Repeat steps 5 and 6 on opposite end of zipper. Slide zipper pulls above marks. Bar tack by zigzagging in place over coil at each placement mark to secure ends of zipper.

8) Press under ½" (1.3 cm) seam allowance on lower edge of each strip. Position folded edges along center of zipper teeth, right sides up; pin. Using zipper foot, topstitch ⅜" (1 cm) from folds.

9) Baste welting to long raw edges of bumper pad cover, using zipper foot. To eliminate bulk, pull out and cut off about 1" (2.5 cm) of cording from ends of welting.

10) Stitch centers of long ties securely to right side of outside bumper pad piece at each of three seams, just below welting. Stitch remaining ties at centers of long side sections.

(Continued on next page)

How to Sew a Bumper Pad (continued)

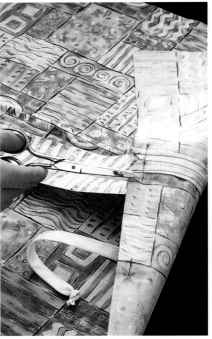

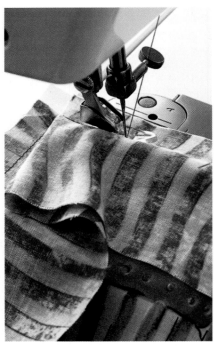

11) Pin short tie to center of each end of outside bumper pad piece, aligning raw edges; stitch.

12) Center short end of boxing strip over end of zipper. Stitch ½" (1.3 cm) seam starting and stopping ½" (1.3 cm) from edges of boxing strip; backstitch at each end. Clip side pieces to corners.

13) Open zipper partway. Pin one edge of boxing strip, right sides together, to the edges of outside bumper pad; clip at corners. Stitch, with boxing side up; pivot at upper corners and end at backstitching. Repeat for other side.

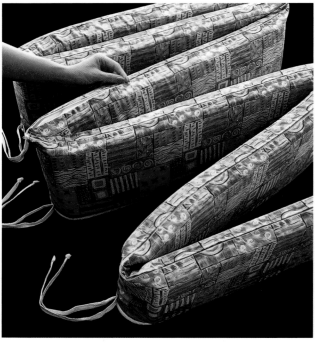

14) Pin inside and outside bumper pad layers together at vertical seamlines and centers of long sides. Stitch as pinned, starting and stopping about 2" (5 cm) from top and bottom of the bumper pad.

15) Place foam inserts into bumper pad. Zip closed. Tie onto crib.

Fitted Crib Sheets

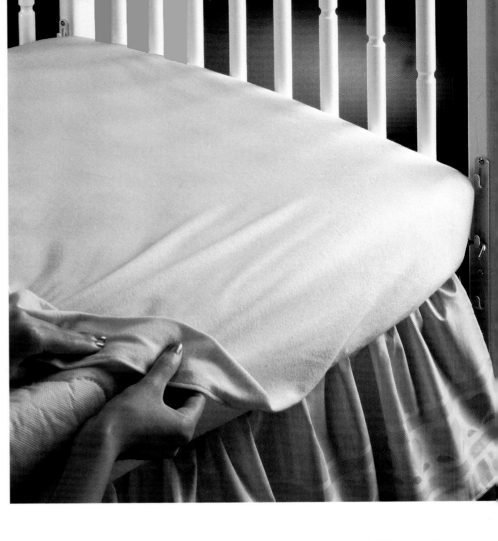

Fitted crib sheets can be coordinated with accessories such as bumper pads or coverlets. Interlock or jersey knit fabrics work best for comfort and stretchability.

Determine the fabric requirement for the size of your mattress. The fabric width equals the mattress width plus two times the depth plus 6" (15 cm) for seam allowances and fitted edge. The fabric length equals the mattress length plus two times the mattress depth plus 6" (15 cm). The square that is cut from each corner equals the mattress depth plus 3" (7.5 cm).

To fit a mattress of 27"×52"×5" (68.5×132×12.5 cm) for a six-year crib, cut a 43" × 68" (109 × 173 cm) rectangle from 2 yd. (1.85 m) of 60" (152.5 cm) wide knit fabric. The width of the sheet should be on the crosswise grain or the grain with the greatest amount of stretch. Cut an 8" (20.5 cm) square from each corner.

How to Sew a Fitted Crib Sheet

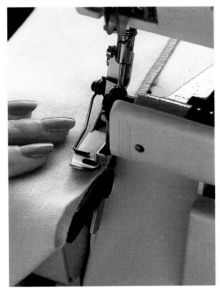

1) Cut square from each corner of sheet, as directed above. Fold sheet at each corner, with the right sides together and raw edges even. Stitch ¼" (6 mm) corner seam on a serger or use a narrow zigzag stitch on a conventional machine.

2) Cut two strips of ¼" (6 mm) wide elastic 3" (7.5 cm) less than width of mattress. On wrong side of sheet, pin center of elastic to center of each short end of sheet. Pin ends of elastic 6" (15 cm) beyond corner seams.

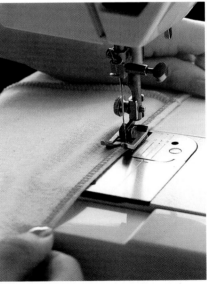

3) Serge or zigzag elastic to the raw edges, as in step 2, page 58. Continue stitching on edges between ends of elastic to finish all raw edges. Turn ¼" (6 mm) hem to wrong side of sheet, encasing elastic. Topstitch hem, stretching elastic.

Crib Coverlets

Prequilted panels make the construction of a crib coverlet easy. These printed panels are about 45" (115 cm) wide and 36" (91.5 cm) long. Prequilted fabrics may also be used. Fabric layers usually include a cotton/polyester top fabric that is quilted to polyester batting. The backing may be brushed nylon tricot or a coordinating print or solid fabric of the same fiber content as the top fabric. To finish the panel edges, use either a pregathered trim and single-fold bias tape or a coordinating ruffle with attached bias tape.

Purchase the trim 5" (12.5 cm) longer than the distance around the panel. For easy application of the trim, round all corners of the coverlet, using a dinner plate to form the curve. Stitch around the coverlet a scant ¼" (6 mm) from the edges to secure the cut quilting threads and to make it easier to apply the trim.

How to Apply Pregathered Trim and Bias Tape

1) Pin trim on panel, with wrong side of trim facing underside of panel, beginning near one corner. Curve end of trim into seam allowance so ends overlap and finished edges taper to raw edge. Ease extra fullness into ruffle at corners, so ruffle lies flat when turned.

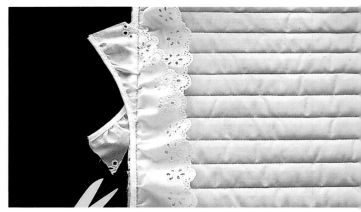

2) Stitch ¼" (6 mm) from raw edge (as shown) around panel to beginning of trim. Curve end of trim into seam allowance so ends overlap and finished edges taper to raw edge. Trim ends of pregathered trim even with panel edge.

How to Apply a Ruffle with Attached Bias Tape

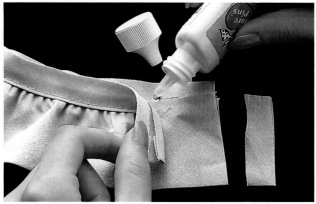

1) Remove stitching for 1½" (3.8 cm) on bias tape. Trim excess ruffle even with bias tape. Press ½" (1.3 cm) of ruffle and both tapes to inside. Glue-baste tapes to both sides of ruffle.

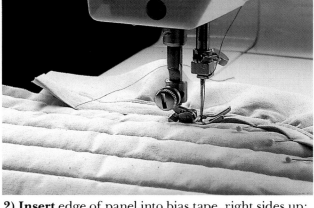

2) Insert edge of panel into bias tape, right sides up; pin. (Narrower bias tape or side with most attractive stitching is right side of trim.) Edgestitch tape to panel, beginning 1" (2.5 cm) from end of tape.

3) Stitch to within 2" (5 cm) from end. Cut excess trim, leaving ½" (1.3 cm); insert into the folded end of trim.

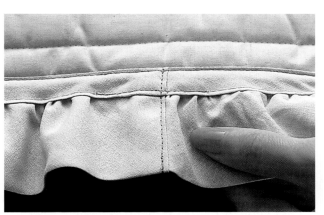

4) Finish stitching tape to panel, overlapping previous stitches. Stitch unstitched portion of other edge of tape, overlapping original stitching. Edgestitch ruffle and tape together at opening.

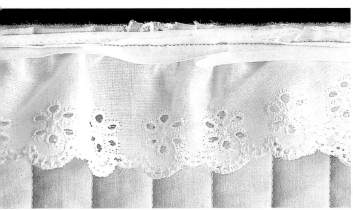

3) Open ½" (1.3 cm) single-fold bias tape; fold under ¼" (6 mm) at one end. Place tape foldline over trim, right sides together, on previous stitching; stitch in crease. Lap tape ½" (1.3 cm) over folded end to finish.

4) Turn tape to right side of panel, encasing raw edges of trim and panel. (It may be necessary to trim seam allowances.) Pin tape in place. Edgestitch free edge of tape to panel, matching needle thread color to tape, and bobbin thread to underside of panel.

Wall Sculptures

Dress up the walls of the nursery with padded fabric sculptures. Choose simple outline designs from paper cutouts or coloring books, or use any of the designs on page 121; add details with machine stitching or appliqués. Enlarge the designs as necessary, using a copy machine or graph paper.

Personalize the room by spelling out the child's name in bright padded letters. Enlarge the letters on page 120 to 12" (30.5 cm) for a wall display, or enlarge them to 4" (10 cm) for a smaller ribbon-tied garland to hang on the door or outside the crib.

Select a firmly woven, mediumweight fabric for the front of the sculpture and a coordinating or matching fabric for the back. Interline the sculptures with ¼" (6 mm) polyurethane foam for firm support or with 6-oz. (175 g) upholstery batting for a more plush look.

✂ Cutting Directions

Cut rectangles for the front, back, and interlining slightly larger than the pattern. Trace the mirror image of the pattern on the wrong side of the front. Transfer any design marks to the right side.

YOU WILL NEED

Fabric for front.

Coordinating or matching fabric for back.

Polyurethane foam, ¼" (6 mm) thick or 6-oz. (175 g) upholstery batting, for interlining.

Small plastic rings, for hanging.

How to Make a Wall Sculpture

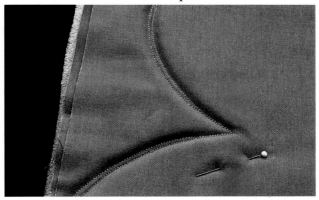

1) Fuse any appliqués to front. Pin front and back, right sides together, over interlining. Stitch on marked outline. Stitch second row of stitches just outside first row; at corners, taper stitches into first stitching line.

2) Trim fabric away to within ⅛" (3 mm) of stitches. Clip to stitching line at corners. Cut 3" (7.5 cm) slit through interlining and back; turn right side out.

3) Push out corners, using point turner. Press lightly. Cut 4" (10 cm) strip of fusible interfacing, 1" (2.5 cm) wide; slip under slit, and fuse closed.

4) Straight-stitch around any appliqués; stitch other design lines and add other embellishments as desired. Hand-stitch one or more plastic rings near top to hang.

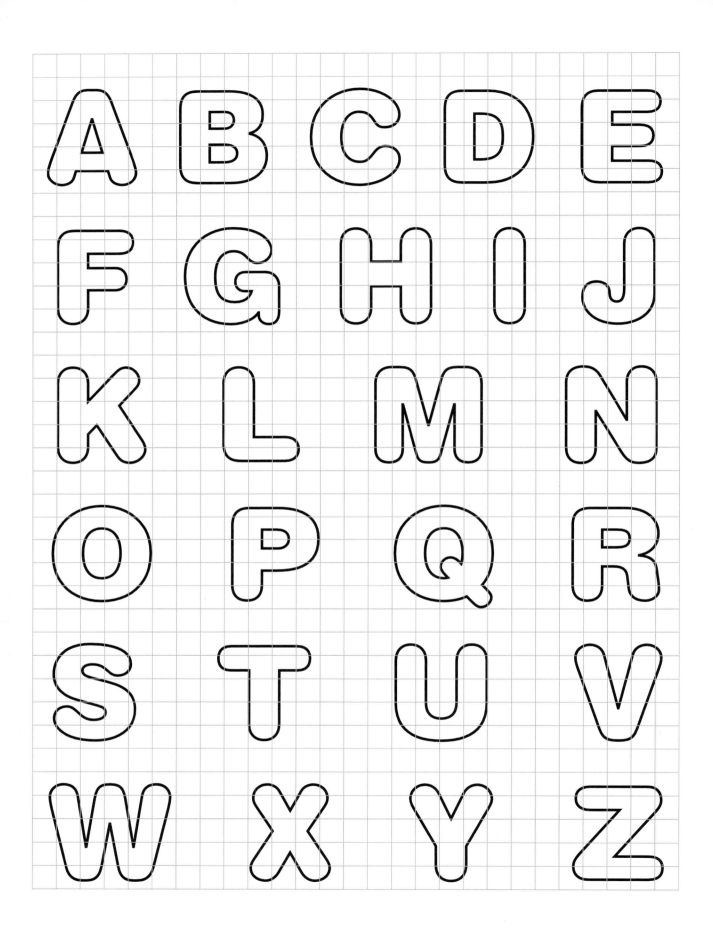

Creative Window Toppers

Simple lined rectangles are transformed into adorable window toppers. All you need is a little imagination. Because the topper hangs flat, it requires minimal fabric, but with a little creativity, it becomes the focal point of the wall. Add some personality with appliqués (pages 94 to 97), sewn to the outer fabric before constructing the topper. Sew padded shapes, following the directions for wall sculptures, page 119. Attach them to the topper after construction, using machine or hand stitching. Accent the topper with colorful buttons and beads.

For a dimensional effect, add batting between the layers, and quilt around the design in the fabric or quilt your own design. Or create interest at the lower edge of the topper with scallops, notches, or points.

Attach the window topper to a decorative rod or pole with sew-on or clip-on rings or ribbon ties. Position the rod above the window so that the upper edge of the topper will just cover the upper edge of the window frame.

✂ Cutting Directions

Cut the outer fabric and lining with the length and width equal to the desired finished length and width plus 1" (2.5 cm) for ½" (1.3 cm) seam allowances on all sides. If piecing is necessary, use one full width of fabric and add equal partial widths to each side, matching the pattern, if any. For a quilted topper, cut batting to the same size as the fabric. Cut ribbon ties, 24" (61 cm) long, if desired.

YOU WILL NEED

Decorator fabric.

Coordinating fabric for lining.

Resin-bonded lightweight polyester batting, for quilted topper.

Decorative rod.

Sew-on or clip-on rings, for basic topper.

Grosgrain ribbon, ⅞" (2.2 cm) wide, for ribbon-tied topper; 24" (61 cm) per tie.

How to Sew a Basic Window Topper

1) Pin outer fabric to lining, right sides together, matching raw edges. Stitch ½" (1.3 cm) seams around all sides; leave 8" (20.5 cm) opening along one side for turning. Trim corners diagonally.

2) Turn back and press seam allowances in opening. Insert seam roll, heavy cardboard tube, or wooden dowel into the opening; press seam allowances open. Turn right side out. Stitch opening closed.

3) Attach sew-on or pin-on rings, spacing them evenly 6" to 8" (15 to 20.5 cm) apart, with one at each end.

How to Sew a Topper with Ribbon Ties

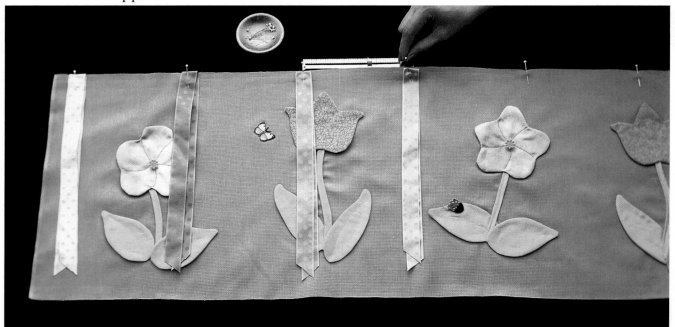

Mark placement for end ties 1" (2.5 cm) from sides of top edge of outer fabric. Mark placement for other ties between marks, evenly spaced 6" to 8" (15 to 20 cm) apart. Fold ties in half; center one tie over each mark, aligning folds to top edge of fabric; pin. Stitch ties in place, ⅜" (1 cm) from edge. Complete topper as above, steps 1 to 3. Take care not to catch ribbon tails in stitching.

How to Sew a Quilted Window Topper

1) Mark quilting design on outer fabric, if necessary; use light pencil marks or removable marker. Baste batting to wrong side of outer fabric scant ½" (1.3 cm) from outer edge. Attach ribbon ties, opposite, if desired. Follow step 1 for basic topper, opposite; trim batting close to stitching. Follow step 2.

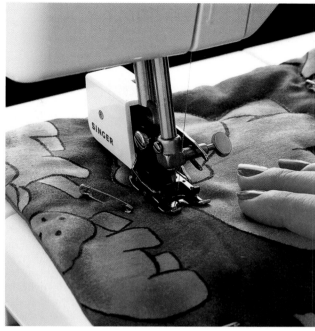

2) Baste layers together, using safety pins. Machine-quilt on marked lines or around shapes in fabric design, using an Even Feed® foot. Remove safety pins. Attach rings or tie ribbons.

How to Shape the Lower Edge

1) Draw desired shaping line for lower edge on wrong side of outer fabric; add ½" (1.3 cm) seam allowances. Attach ribbon ties, opposite, if desired.

2) Continue as in step 1, opposite. Clip to stitching line along curves and inside corners; trim diagonally at outside corners. Finish as in steps 2 and 3.

Index

Creative Publishing international, Inc.
offers a variety of how-to books. For
information write:
  Creative Publishing international, Inc.
  Subscriber Books
  5900 Green Oak Drive
  Minnetonka, MN 55343